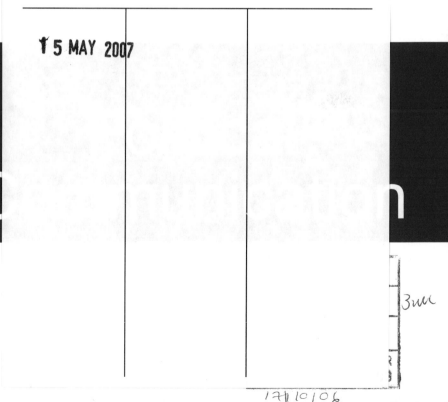

Recent volumes include:

Key Concepts in Social Research
Geoff Payne and Judy Payne

Fifty Key Concepts in Gender Studies
Jane Pilcher and Imelda Whelehan

Key Concepts in Medical Sociology
Jonathan Gabe, Mike Bury and Mary Ann Elston

Key Concepts in Leisure Studies
David Harris

Key Concepts in Critical Social Theory
Nick Crossley

Key Concepts in Urban Studies
Mark Gottdiener and Leslie Budd

Key Concepts in Mental Health
David Pilgrim

Key Concepts in Journalism Studies
Bob Franklin, Martin Hamer, Mark Hanna, Marie Kinsey and John Richardson

The SAGE Key Concepts series provides students with accessible and authoritative knowledge of the essential topics in a variety of disciplines. Cross-referenced throughout, the format encourages critical evaluation through understanding. Written by experienced and respected academics, the books are indispensable study aids and guides to comprehension.

DARREN G. LILLEKER

Key Concepts in
Political
Communication

SAGE Publications
London ● Thousand Oaks ● New Delhi

First published 2006

SAGE Publications Ltd
1 Oliver's Yard
55 City Road
London EC1Y 1SP

SAGE Publications Inc
2455 Teller Road
Thousand Oaks, California 91320

SAGE Publications India Pvt Ltd
B-42 Panchsheel Enclave
Post Box 4109
New Delhi 110 017

British Library Cataloguing in Publication data

A catalogue record for this book is
available from the British Library

ISBN 1 4129 1830 8
ISBN 1 4129 1831 6 (pbk)

Library of Congress control number: 2005928592

Typeset by M Rules
Printed on paper from sustainable resources
Printed in Great Britain by Cromwell Press Ltd, Trowbridge, Wilts

contents

**political
communication**

v

preface and dedication

The idea for this book came from students at Bournmouth University taking the Political Communication option of a BA communication degree. They were new to politics, yet familiar with many of the terms and ideas, but what they lacked was a textbook that introduced the core concepts of the field of study in their context. I would like to thank them for the idea, and some of the 2004/5 cohort for reading through the concepts to ensure they serve their purpose. I would also like to acknowledge those who brought to discussions ideas that helped broaden my thinking on some of the concepts.

I owe gratitude to all the researchers in the field of political communication whose work has informed my own research and the work herein. I would also like to recognise the support offered by Jamilah Ahmed, Fabienne Pedroletti and Julia Hall at Sage; their enthusiasm for this project was hugely helpful throughout the process. Finally, I thank Teresa for her enduring love, support and patience.

I dedicate this book to my son Mark and my daughters Kayleigh and Yazmin; you were constant distractions throughout the writing process, but I love you all for that.

Darren G. Lilleker, Poole 2005

political communication

vii

Introduction

Communication between the ruling organisations of a society and the people is central to any political system. However, in a democracy, political communication is seen as crucial for the building of a society where the state and its people feel they are connected. Political communication must, therefore, perform the role of an activator; it cannot simply be a series of edicts to society from the elite, ruling group but must allow feedback from society and encourage participation. While some may argue that a regular vote is sufficient for a nation to be termed democratic, this could also be described as a dictatorship with a finite term. Modern democracies need to be increasingly responsive to their publics, and at the heart of responsiveness is a dialogue. Classic definitions of political communication focus on the source and the motivation; political communication flows out from the political sphere and must have a political purpose. However, such definitions would not be completely appropriate for many modern states, particularly given the role of the media. Therefore modern texts focus on three actors, some of whom operate beyond the boundaries of any single state, each of whom produce political communication. These are, firstly, the political sphere itself: the state and its attendant political actors. Their role is to communicate their actions to society in order to gain legitimacy among and compliance from the people. Secondly, there are the non-state actors, where we would include a range of organisations with political motivations as well as corporate bodies and, of course, the voters. Each of these organisations and groups communicate messages into the political sphere, in the hope of having some level of influence. Finally, there are the media outlets, the media communicates about politics, influencing the public as well as the political spheres. In a free, open and pluralist society, on which the majority of texts concentrate, each of these communicates independently but synergistically with one another. In other words, they say what they want when they want but are influenced by one another and may well be led by one particular group when formulating arguments, opinions, policies, perceptions or attitudes.

Despite the academic study of political communication being a fairly young discipline; the actual practice is as old as politics itself. Just as Pope Innocent III ordered his minions in England in 1213 to nail what was known as a papal bull, a poster bearing the seal of the pope, to church doors informing the English of the excommunication of their king, John; modern politicians use all the available media to deliver messages to the people. The example of King John's excommunication is pertinent, albeit dated, as this was one of many times when there were forces competing for the support of the people. The Catholic Church used the best method for disseminating a message among faithful churchgoers, the majority of English society at that time, informing them that their king, and therefore kingdom, was no longer recognised by the Church: keep the king and go to hell was the inference. The message was also designed as a warning to King John that another, more suitable, ruler, Philip Augustus, king of France, was allowed sanction to invade. Such communication is prevalent across the world today, between states and within states, at the heart of which is persuasion: that the receiver should act in a way desired by the sender.

Within modern democracies the people elect a person, and usually their party, to run the country for a defined period of time, usually between four and five years. In order that the people can make the choice of who to elect, each competitor must communicate to them effectively. Each competitor tries to persuade the public that they, at what ever level they are standing, from national president to town mayor, are the best for the job. Subsequently, when one or another individual or party is elected, it is essential that they continue to communicate. Some would argue that this communication is central to encouraging democratic culture; it is the provision of information that is required by the people (Denton and Woodward, 1990). However, there are more cynical accounts which argue that the majority of communication from the elected is designed to retain support among the electorate for their policies, what has been termed as 'manufacturing consent' (Herman and Chomsky, 1998). Therefore political communication is often placed central to debates on the health and well-being of our democracy and the styles and levels of interaction are often used as a measure of the strength of public approval and engagement in the political system (Blumler and Gurevitch, 1995).

In an ideal world scenario political communication is unproblematic. However, due to a range of developments in the political, social and technological spheres political communication has been forced to change, both in style and in substance. Furthermore, across all democracies, there are a greater number of political voices, both elective and non-elective, competing for the ear of the public. This makes political communication an increasingly complex business, not only as an area of academic study but also in the way it is practiced. This introduction will provide an overview of the types of political communication, their functions and the motivations of those who communicate political messages. The introduction introduces the key concepts explained throughout the book so allowing an understanding of how each concept fits with the context of political communication. Prior to this, however, it is useful to explain the context of democratic politics.

THE DEMOCRATIC STATE

Democratic states are defined by the institutionalisation of free, fair and regular elections that do not debar anyone from participating, whether as voters or candidates, on grounds that are unreasonable: in the 21st century these would include race and ethnic background, gender and political beliefs. Those we elect are our representatives; they use their political power, given by the people through the vote, on behalf of the people. This is the fundamental concept of a representative democracy: to ensure a broad range of people, and their views, are represented; made possible by both state and society supporting pluralism of views and access to the media. Pluralism allows power to be widely dispersed across a number of political groupings with contrasting views, all of whom have access to a largely neutral governmental machine. There are debates on the effectiveness of this system (see Heywood, 1997: 65–82); however, the twin principles of democracy and pluralism predominate in the world.

In a representative democratic state there are various tiers, or levels, of political power. Broadly speaking these can be separated between national and local; however, there are state differences. Some states have at the head of the political system a president, and beneath the president an elected chamber of representatives; these two levels should ensure power is not centralised. Other systems have a parliament led by a prime minister and cabinet government whose party holds power over legislation (lawmaking) but is responsible and accountable to a larger group of representatives, often from a range of other political parties. Below the national government there are a range of regional and/or local tiers of government. These are responsible to national government but are often also elected. Outside of the elected political structure are pressure groups representing those voters who share a single special interest; they can be representatives of workers in one industry, such as trade unions or professional associations, or they may be businesses or industrial representatives. These all compete for representation within the political system and can often be brought into the process of decision making (Grant, 1989). Communication from and between these groups is essential to the health of democracy, though the diffusion of power can mean that their views can remain marginalized and they may be forced to take action that gains them greater attention than they would normally be awarded: workers can withdraw their labour, interest groups can hold demonstrations, marginalized groups can resort to terror tactics. The latter can all be indications of a failure within the system of a pluralist, representative democracy and are a recurrent feature of the modern world.

One further powerful group exists outside of the political system: the broadcast and print media, collectively known as 'the media'. The media act both as the communicator of political views from all groups in a state and as a watchdog that calls political actors to account for their actions. Their role in society has been both attacked and defended by academics, politicians and journalists alike. Some argue the media is too powerful and promotes an agenda that can be contrary to the interests of a pluralist democracy (Entman, 1996). Alternatively, Norris (2000) argues that the media play an important role in upholding the democratic nature of a society and strengthening pluralism. Others take the view that the media can fall under political control, and so weaken pluralism through offering a biased perspective (Reeves, 1997; Wring, 2001). Finally, there is the view that the media report only what they feel is important, that through the selection of news values, framing and agenda-setting, the public fail to receive sufficient information on which to base their voting decision and some views become excluded due to their lack of fit to the media frames, agendas and values (Schlesinger, 1983; Blumler and Gurevitch, 1995; Said, 2000). What all these accounts agree on is the power of the media in determining what is communicated and what is not, what the public know and what they do not know; thus we hear of a media-centred democracy. The greater the independence enjoyed by the media does not equate to reductions in criticisms from all these perspectives, thus central to most studies of political communication, global or national, is a study of the media due to its centrality to the process of the dissemination of political views, information and knowledge.

It is within this context that these concepts will be explained. These are the individuals and groups we expect to be involved in the process of political communication and, based on their roles, we see a central concern among all actors with 'being heard': by each other, by select groups of actors or members of the public, by the mass audience, or by everyone within a society or indeed beyond.

THE HISTORY AND METHODS OF POLITICAL COMMUNICATION

Political communication is as old as political activity; it was a feature of ancient Greece and the Roman Empire as well as across diverse political systems in the modern age. It is hard to think of a time, under any political system, where political leaders have not had a requirement to communicate with other groups in society, or have not had to persuade the people to support them, often as opposed to rivals for their power and position. However, for much of human history political communication would have been a linear, top-down process from leaders to people. This is shown in Figure 1. We see the direction of communication being straight down, the majority being caught by the media and then channelled out once again, what is now referred to as the process of mediation; however little communication was to go from the bottom of society into the political sphere.

Democratisation of the majority of the political systems changed the nature of political communication and political activity moved into the public sphere. The people became involved in politics because they were expected to have a political role. Equally, with increased access to information and greater levels of education, came a demand for greater political involvement and influence. The voter was not content with the simple act of voting, the voter became an active citizen, one who could join an anti-state cause, the fight against apartheid in South Africa for example, as easily as a recognised political party. Communication between the various groups, electoral and non-electoral, became competitive; each vying for space in the media and the attention of the people. Thus we find more complex models for understanding modern political communication.

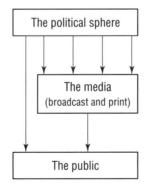

Figure 1   *A traditional view of political communication*

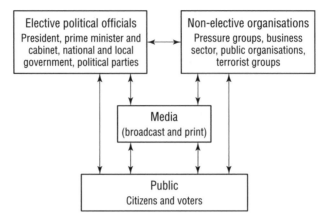

Figure 2   *The Levels of Political Communication*

Figure 2 demonstrates the lines of communication that, theoretically, are open between each group. How communication is made may vary, and how audible the message is can be dependent upon the size of any group or level of support for a party, group or cause and the tactics used to get the message across. However, in a pluralist society, at least in theory, all groups will communicate among themselves and between one another and will be both learning from and competing with one another.

The greater the number of voices competing, the more intense the competition, the better communicators groups must be in order to be heard. Thus we hear of the professionalisation of political communication, that it has become better in some way in order to be heard by more groups and individuals (Mancini, 1999). Some attribute developments purely to learning from practice in the United States (US), others shy away from the Americanisation thesis; however, most agree that the process by which political communication is carried out has evolved, become more technically and technologically sophisticated and adopted techniques from the worlds of corporate advertising and marketing in order to compete in the modern information-rich society.

An early and effective form of direct, or non-mediated, political communication involved public meetings; political campaigners would go out and meet the workers and deliver speeches to them. It was using these tactics that movements like Lenin's Bolsheviks gained the support necessary to undermine Russia's tsar, Nicholas II; equally such meetings allowed the British Labour Party to become an electoral force. Elsewhere, public meetings, in church halls, cinemas or back rooms of hotels, cafes and drinking houses became a key way to meet the people; the memoirs of many democratic politicians, active in the 19th and early 20th century, recall such events during their early careers. The late, veteran United Kingdom (UK) Labour Member of Parliament (MP) Ian Mikardo recalls in his autobiography *Backbencher* a meeting in the canteen of the Miles aircraft factory at Woodley, just outside Reading, the constituency Mikardo successfully fought in 1945. Here he faced 6,000 workers, all worried about redundancies following the end of the Second World War. To secure their votes, Mikardo had to allay their fears while the workers tried to 'squeeze all they could out of the first opportunity they'd had in ten years to put some aspiring politician through the hoop' (Mikardo, 1988: 83). Such meetings are now few and mainly limited to countries where technology does not allow for the message to be delivered directly to homes: the only comparable types of event are the mass rallies held around US presidential elections, or mass meetings of party members.

Technology, however, not only effected political communication in the 20th century. The invention of the printing press allowed Thomas More to attack the inequality in 15th-century England. Since then, every political activist has published pamphlets and often delivered them by hand door to door or placed them in venues where the masses may be reached. While still the preserve of weakly-funded, often radical or underground movements, or those with little access to mass communication media, such activities still take place. Every election across the democratic world will see leafleting, and many argue that such activities are of ultra-importance in determining the result of elections (see particularly the research of David Denver (Denver and Hands, 1997; Denver et al., 2002; see also Johnston, 1987; Negrine and Lilleker, 2003)). But, largely, political communication has become an activity aimed at a mass audience using the mass media of television across the majority of the states in the world today. Hence direct political communication has become less of a feature in recent elections, despite research that indicates the importance of face-to-face interaction between politician and public (Jackson and Lilleker, 2004).

As communications technology allowed mass communication, communication necessarily changed. Many politicians took an instant dislike to the constraints of television: war leaders Winston Churchill and Charles de Gaulle found it hard to adapt their styles and appeared awkward and aloof in front of the camera (Scammell, 1995). They, and many politicians of their era, had learned how to use radio effectively. In fact, during the Second World War, a secondary communication war took place with national leaders transmitting to their own people, to rally support, while enemies attempted to undermine their efforts by broadcasting into other states. Consider the effect on the people of Sheffield, UK, when the Nazi-supporting broadcaster Lord Haw Haw would ask them to look out of their windows and see if 'the ten tall chimneys [of the British Steel factory] were still standing. Do you see them ablaze,' he would mockingly ask. The US-sponsored Radio Free Europe played a similar role when broadcasting into the Soviet bloc during the cold war. Broadcasts would discuss the oppressive nature of Soviet rule and try to encourage dissidence. Few political communicators still use radio as the main means of dissemination, though it still offers politicians potential to reach the people. In the modern age, politicians across the globe have adapted to television and use it in the same way as previous generations used mass rallies. During the 2003 Iraq War, the US government set up a dedicated Arabic-speaking television news service in order to gain support within the Middle East, as this was deemed the most appropriate way to reach this audience. Television, however, is independent in most democratic nations and so is able to mediate political communication, and the political communicator cannot ensure that their message reaches the public unaltered or without editorial comment.

The only groups who appear able to circumnavigate the editorial are those groups whose message is so shocking that the public receive it in such clarity that editorial is wasted. Hence it is appropriate to discuss direct action as the most powerful form of political communication. The crashing of two planes into the World Trade Center and the Pentagon on 9 September 2001, which has become known as 9/11, demonstrated the power of direct action. The events, transmitted live as they unfolded, delivered the message of the terrorists to a global audience (McNair, 2003: 182–4) and spoke of the determination of a small cell of activists to make their voice heard, of the powerlessness of the global community to silence them, and brought to the fore debates surrounding US policy within the Middle East. While these events did not change politics in the US, apart perhaps from forcing a more right-wing approach to foreign policy, suicide bombers on a number of commuter trains in Madrid, Spain, on 11 March 2004 did affect a change of government in the subsequent elections. Such events surpass the marches organised by activists against nuclear weapons and a range of causes, the activities of pressure groups such as Greenpeace or the actions of the average terrorist. However, all these events rely on reaching a mass audience. Few in the world knew of the massacres exacted by Saladin against the crusaders during the 12th century, but television brings modern day equivalents into everybody's homes and lives. Thus the action is perhaps of lesser importance than the attention it draws from the media: it seems all too obvious to state that political communication is usually measured by its ability to receive the right media coverage by whatever means possible.

The media, thus, play an important role in political communication. Media outlet's editors not only choose what to broadcast as news, or how that is reported, but also choose the way it portrays groups in society. Popular culture not only reflects society but also has the power to shape people's political views. The portrayal of political institutions can inform; however, it could also undermine the political system, or one individual or group. Drama can portray the real-life operations of the White House in series like *The West Wing*; caricature the professional and family life of the UK Prime Minister, for example in *My Dad's the Prime Minister*; or follow a tradition of offering a satirical yet critical view of political events, such as in the BBC's *That Was The Week That Was* or *Have I Got News For You*. In an era when it is argued few pursue political information, the blending of politics and popular culture becomes an important source of political knowledge (Street, 1997; 2001).

In the age of mass communication via the moving image, many political actors, with a range of goals, have recognised the great potential that television offers. As film was used to make a political point, particularly in Nazi Germany and in the USSR under Stalin, as well as in many anti-Soviet war films produced in Hollywood, so television is used as a tool of political communication. Arguably this has changed political campaigning. Enabled by the Internet and 24/7 (twenty-four hours a day, seven days a week) news coverage, the public have greater access; they also appear to demand to 'look inside the souls' of those who compete for votes (Coleman, 2003). Rather than the talking head shots that were popular, and all that were possible, during the 1950s and 1960s, politicians now create elaborate montages of images to transmit not just a political message but an image to the public; politics takes on an aesthetic and emotional quality (Street, 1997; Pels, 2003). Equally advertising is used to great effect, particularly by presidential candidates both in the USA and in Russia, where it is used to promote the sponsor and undermine their opposition. Russia's President Vladimir Putin enjoyed virtual monopoly control over the largest broadcasting stations, and it is his ability to transmit his message through every element of television coverage that some look to when explaining his 1999 landslide victory and subsequent hold over political power (Belin, 2001).

Political communication has then moved from being a direct, personal, face-to-face, activity to being conducted indirectly via the media of mass communication. However, in many ways, the style of communication has come full circle. One British candidate for parliament recalled that people liked public meetings because 'when they asked an awkward question they liked to see if you sweated or not', he claimed, 'because on television everyone is very prepared and it's staged.' However, debates between US presidential candidates, programmes like the BBC's *Question Time* or the appearances of New Zealand Prime Minister Helen Clark on talk shows, provide the same scrutiny. Preparedness is seen as part of the 'professionalisation' of political communication, an issue that will be returned to when discussing many of the concepts; however, the public still appear to demand to see whether their would-be political representatives sweat. It is this battle over image that makes political communication a fascinating area of study as politicians attempt to use the media as a multifunctional political communications tool.

However, political communication, as noted in Figure 2, is not all top down. The political communication audience, defined often as both citizens and voters, is able to communicate to political groups, sometimes through membership or lobbying, and to and via the media. Direct action is one powerful method the public use, and in forming political groups to further causes increases the scope of pluralism. The Internet has allowed groups to communicate effectively, stage highly effective and visible events and so gain significant media attention (Rodgers, 2004). However, other and more ordinary methods are used. The letters to the media can lead an agenda as well as fit within the news values (Franklin, 2004: 168–9). But the most reported form of public political communication are opinion polls (Moon, 1999), which are used to gauge support for causes, political parties, groups and policies as well as predict election results. They are also used by politicians, to some extent, to determine what courses of action can be pursued and those that cannot.

THE FUNCTIONS OF POLITICAL COMMUNICATION IN CONTEXT

So, political communication is conducted through every channel and media available, it is multifarious and multifaceted, and it is inescapable. But what is the purpose of this continual bombardment of information, views, opinions and debates? At the most simplistic and obvious level, political communication is all about winning over others (Moloney, 2001). We know that electoral candidates want to win votes, but also dictators want to win the love of their people, cause groups and activists want to win attention; the public want a say, it is perhaps as simple as that. However, this can suggest a somewhat cynical view of politics and really means that all political communication is nothing more than propaganda. Political communication is reduced to 'winning over' or persuading others, and solely concerned with the acquisition of power: whether governmental power or power over the media agenda. Even so, there are a range of contextual factors that alter the role that the message plays.

If we firstly take the organisations seeking electoral support, the parties and candidates, their communication has a different role for different circumstances. If any group or individual seeking election could separate out groups of people in society, and talk to each group on an individual basis, electoral political communication would be simple. However, a speech by a presidential candidate in any country is transmitted to anyone and everyone. Therefore, that piece of communication must serve a range of functions: make the candidate appear in touch with the majority of voters; heal rifts between social groups or classes; show that groups will not be excluded; make the candidate appear to identify with the people. This means it cannot be purely cynically produced propaganda, particularly as the 21st-century voter in the majority of liberal democracies is a sophisticated political animal and cannot be fooled easily. Political communication is further complicated in nations where coalition governments are common. Party leaders in Germany, for example, find that a priority is to communicate the right message not only to their own supporters or voters but to potential coalition partners and their supporters and voters (Lees, 2005). This makes the above list of roles longer and, of course, the communication much harder to design.

These functions are appropriate within the confines of the state; however, communication is rarely locked within national borders. Austrian presidential candidate Jorge Haider capitalised on populist nationalism and opposition to immigration to openly campaign for repatriation of 'non-Austrians' during his 2000 election campaign. This won him a landslide victory, but following his election he found that relations were strained with Austria's partners in the European Union and that leaders openly discussed whether economic sanctions should be placed against his regime. While the crisis for Austria ended without sanction, helped by (as well as helping) the Haider government's quick collapse, this was caused by a lack of consideration for the international reception of communication aimed at one segment of the Austrian electorate. A translator employed by a European state during a state visit by Russian President Boris Yeltsin recalled an alternative example. Prior to Yeltsin's arrival, and when he was not around, Yeltsin was referred to by the insulting moniker that roughly translated as 'the drunken tramp'. In stark contrast every official statement commended his bravery during the demise of the Communist regime, his statesmanship and any other attribute that would nurture a long and friendly relationship between the two countries. The latter is a common form of interstate political communication of course: diplomacy.

While we can clearly see an argument for describing these examples as intending to gain support, there is an additional informative function. The public have to be informed of new legislation, how they are affected, and how they can comply. There are also a range of other forms of informative communication that come under the heading of 'public information', where the attention may well be to persuade but not for political motives. Here we include information regarding social benefits, health campaigns, public awareness of dangers and any communication designed to inform rather than influence politically. There is of course a blurring of boundaries here (Franklin, 2004). New legislation can be communicated in such a way that government also promotes itself, as caring, competent or proactive, hence we hear of the permanent campaiging of the public relations state (Davis, 2002). Similar comments can and are often made regarding public information; however, the key function of this form of communication should not be to gain support.

Of course any new legislation may be received differently by the range of audiences, both internal and external. Economic policy announcements by any member of the European Union, or the Organisation of Petroleum Exporting Countries (OPEC), may well have repercussions upon partners within the organisations as well as trading partners globally. Thus such policies have to be communicated in a way that allays fears so avoiding a loss of economic confidence. Equally, as any government often operates within utilitarian parameters, constructing policies that will have the best long-term effects for the majority of citizens, these benefits must be communicated and again fears allayed, particularly towards stakeholder groups, whose support is important, but also to minority groups that may feel marginalized. All these contextual issues must be considered when communication is constructed, thus when we study political communication we have to consider all the intended functions across all the different audiences that will receive the message.

The different levels of politics, local, national and supranational, may compete for power and influence. The European Court of Justice has found member states' governments to have acted unlawfully, causing competing claims for justice by state nationals on the one hand and debates regarding state sovereignty on the other. Equally, national and local governments can come into conflict over taxation powers for example; as can different arms of government. Nations where there are two houses, a bicameral system, both elected as in the USA, France or Russia, or one elected and one appointed as is the case in the UK and Israel, can find conflict between the houses. In the UK the House of Lords scrutinises legislation for problems or errors, it can demand amendments or block legislation, and this system can allow a democratically elected government to be undermined by a non-democratic group of ex-politicians and other elite figures. Both will then argue over their powers, both promoting themselves in order to gain supportive media coverage, and win over public opinion and opinion among the other wing of government.

Beyond the realm of government there are other various tiers in the political hierarchy, each of which communicate to the public. Regional levels of government, such as the German *Land*, the US State government, the UK local and municipal councils or the tribal councils across many African states, often use communication to promote their representative function. This function is also one that is important to members of parliaments who represent distinct geographical areas, such as UK MPs, or Members of the European Parliament (MEPs). Their communication is designed to show that they fulfil a representative function; however, most communication from political actors shares one central feature: the direction of communication is one way from the political to the public. Evidence suggests that this is in contrast to the desires of the people. The global attraction of audience interest and participation in real-life shows has led some to argue that this is the kind of interaction the public want with the political sphere (Coleman, 2003): that they want to be able to shape governmental activity and have direct input to the legislature. This has led to discussion of the emergence of the political consumer, a voter who seeks to have their personal requirements and needs met by government before offering support (Lees-Marshment and Lilleker, 2005). This suggests moving towards a two-way style of communication favoured by public relations theorists (Grunig and Hunt, 1994; Jackson and Lilleker, 2004), where the organisation and the public have an open relationship founded on communication. This currently does not seem to be a function of much political communication.

But what of those who are outside the electoral political system? Pressure groups such as Greenpeace suggest that they talk for 'the future of the world', and their activities are designed to stop the current political and industrial sphere from destroying the earth. The function of their communication, whether direct action reported by the media, the press releases they send to the media or the direct mail or leafleting they engage in, is designed to make people think. It is an accepted notion that no amount of campaigning can directly drive public opinion, but it can influence what the public think about. Many non-electoral groups act in this way, as do other public figures. U2 singer Bono's call for Live Aid 2, what became Live8, a music event to raise awareness of the suffering in the Third World, put the issue on the agenda, as did the original work of musicians Bob Geldof and Midge Ure when organising Live Aid in 1984. It can be argued that because it is a non-electoral actor taking the initiative that it has more credibility and that it is not seen as a cynical manoeuvre for electoral gain. Although it is no bad career move, it would seem that some of these figures act for political and economic motives through non-political channels (Marshall, 1997). This is the function of many groups; however, their communication function is the same – to influence the news agenda.

We could then argue that all communication has one core function: to gain media attention. This would, perhaps, be a fair assessment, but many non-political communicators also seek to control the media reporting of events; thus competition becomes fiercer and media management techniques more sophisticated. However, there is a fine line between informing the public or highlighting an issue and attempting to influence public opinion directly. The former will allow the public to decide for themselves, the latter will largely try to offer no choices. This behaviour is largely the preserve of electoral competitors, it is not something uniform to all those who engage in political communication.

RECEIVING POLITICAL COMMUNICATION

Yet we must not assume that all this communication is received without question or in its entirety. The people are argued to have a lot more power than is realised. They can select what to believe and disbelieve, what to accept or reject, what to view and what to ignore. The people also do not operate in isolation. While they may not all join political groups they socialise, and socialisation can incubate certain political views (Graber, 2001). Within the minds of the citizen voter, then, there are lots of competing views. This is often equated to constant noise reverberating around our brains. Noise is anything else that influences the way the public think about a piece of communication they receive from a political organisation. It can be broadcast political satire, the opinions of workmates and friends, the headline of their newspaper, perhaps even their own ideology. All these can alter the way that the communication is received and whether it is trusted or believed. Noise acts like someone whispering in your ear 'politicians always lie' as you watch a leader's speech on television. Of course some political communication filters through unchecked by the media and may slip beneath the noise of other influences. Which bits filter through and which do not depend on various factors. For example, any news on the 2003/4 conflict in Iraq received a great deal of media attention across all the world's media. Within the minds of each member of the public an opinion developed, influenced possibly by conversations with family members, friends and by their own attitudes to Iraq, war in general or a range of other factors – often whether friends or family could become embroiled in the conflict is important. The point is that little political communication regarding Iraq would have reached the public without being filtered by both the media and by other noise.

Government leaflets, an often used form of direct communication, may grab attention, be trusted as information only and not become distorted by the media, similarly with websites, e-newsletters or other campaign communication that fall under the radar of the media. However, noise is less easy to remove from political communication. Some people are cynical of all political communication; the noise they hear is much greater when listening to a politician speak and will sound like someone screaming 'la la la' to block out the words. At the end of the speech they will not remember anything about it yet happily state 'it was all the usual lies'. Most people are not that mistrustful of politicians, but largely little gets through to the public directly. In fact the usual assumption is that it is only 1 per cent of all communication that reaches the public unfiltered, and of that only about 25 per cent, so 0.25 per cent overall, is remembered. This does not mean that the people remember little about politics, more that they only remember the bits they see as relevant to them. When we consider how much political communication is directed at the audiences, perhaps 0.25 per cent is quite a lot.

The complexities faced by any political organisation when trying to communicate to the public has led to an increasing sophistication and exploitation of any and every communication method and route. However, in many democratic nations, it is argued that politics is in crisis. Apathy rules, the public do not want to listen; politics is viewed as detached from society and politicians often regarded as self-seeking and power hungry egotists. This crisis centres upon the issue of communication. Communication does not only fulfil the practical functions discussed above, communication also projects an image. In this context, politicians try to create a personality for themselves, to be more than just a 'grey man in a grey suit'. Thus US television viewers witnessed

political communication

15

presidential candidate Bill Clinton playing saxophone on mainstream television, Russian President Yeltsin playing the spoons alongside prominent pop bands, UK Prime Minister Tony Blair appearing on the family-oriented and apolitical UK chat show *Des O'Connor Tonight*. These are all examples of image creation. However, communicating political values is more difficult. How can you show you are trustworthy? This is a question that is fundamental within discussions surrounding the future of government, and its communication strategies and organisations, within the early years of the 21st century.

The crisis faced by governments and electoral parties or candidates is not shared by the non-electoral organisations. Despite their single-issue politics, and their clear bias surrounding an issue, they appear to be trusted and more able to communicate their messages to the public. However, those argued to make an impact are figures on the periphery of politics, with celebrity status, who promote political causes. Over the last 50 years television personalities, actors and musicians have taken an increasing role within politics. Few, outside of the USA, actually stand for election, and it is more usual for the celebrity who proclaims political views to have a more subtle role: they create noise people want to hear that could influence the way they think about political issues of the day. Internationally recognised pop stars like Sting or Bono often publicly endorse political campaigns, acting as a lever upon national governments (Marshall, 1997). While effects are often difficult to attribute to one artist or one promotional event, their impact is significant and one that can counter the power of a government. Under circumstances where politicians are mistrusted, the power of the celebrity is increased and the problem exacerbated.

Political organisations try to compete with popular culture and cut through the noise. They produce a range of communication in an attempt to reach their target audiences and nurture support for their views and policies. They use techniques of advertising, marketing and public relations to these ends, but largely are never sure exactly what worked and what failed. It remains almost impossible to understand or measure communication effects in a pluralist democratic society; in fact, Baudrillard's view seems very prescient: 'We will never know if an advertisement or opinion poll has had a real influence on individual or collective will, but we will never know either what would have happened if there had been no opinion poll or advertisement' (1988: 210).

UNDERSTANDING POLITICAL COMMUNICATION

We therefore see that political communication is a complex business both to operate within and to study from outside. There are various types and styles of communication, which are in a state of constant evolution, and that in turn serve different functions among the different communicators and the context of the communication. A range of messages are transmitted, using all available media, to an audience that is largely autonomous and keen to be free of any coercion. We find context to be of great importance in shaping communication; therefore we find ourselves, as students of political communication, having to understand the communicator and the different organisations and peoples being communicated to in order to truly understand the functions and roles of the communication. Political communication theories largely share a common basis that was first developed by Harold Lasswell in a US doctoral dissertation studying propaganda effects; his core question was '*who* says *what* to *whom* via which *channels* with what *effects?*' (Lasswell, 1927). The italicised aspects map neatly to the template which has guided much communication research, see Figure 3.

The four components of communication are each studied, sometimes in isolation from one another, at other times in linear fashion where all components are discussed. This text does not overtly apply this model; however, implicitly it is easy to see how discussion is guided by it. Thus we find a range of discussions on the way the source of political communication is viewed, particularly in terms of their credibility, and how the sources attempt to manage the other three parts of the chain; so managing the perception that audiences hold of them. Similarly we will discuss message construction and the way these are transmitted, necessitating discussions of the role of the independent mass media. Finally the receivers, or audiences, who in reality are centre stage in political communication, feature in terms of the way in which, if at all, they receive, process and then act upon political communication. The discussion will introduce the latest research in order to provide a rounded picture of the field of political communication at the turn of the 21st century.

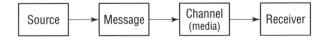

Figure 3   *The classic model of communication*

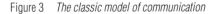

REFERENCES

Baudrillard, J. (1988) *Selected Writings*. Cambridge: Polity Press.

Belin, L. (2001) 'Political bias and self-censorship in the Russian media', in A. Brown. *Contemporary Russian Politics: A Reader*. Oxford: Oxford University Press.

Blumler, J. and Gurevitch, M. (1995) *The Crisis of Public Communication*. London: Routledge.

Coleman, S. (2003) *A Tale of Two Houses: The House of Commons, the Big Brother House and the People at Home*. London: Hansard Society.

Davis, A. (2002) *Public Relations Democracy: Public Relations, Politics and the Mass Media in Britain*. Manchester: Manchester University Press.

Denton, R.E. and Woodward, G.C. (1990) *Political Communication in America*. New York: Praeger.

Denver, D. and Hands, G. (1997) *Modern Constituency Elections*. London: Frank Cass.

Denver, D., Hands, G., Fisher, J. and MacAllister, I. (2002) 'The impact of constituency campaigning in the 2001 General Election', in L. Bennie et al. (eds), *British Elections and Parties Review 12*. London: Frank Cass. pp. 80–94.

Entman, R. (1996) 'Reporting environmental policy debate: the real media biases', *Harvard International Journal of Press/Politics*, 2 (4): 32–51.

Franklin, B. (2004) *Packaging Politics: Political Communications in Britain's Media Democracy*. London: Edward Arnold.

Graber, D. (2001) *Processing Politics: Learning from Television in the Internet Age*. Chicago: University of Chicago Press.

Grant, W. (1989) *Pressure Groups, Politics and Democracy in Britain*. Hemel Hempstead, Philip Allan.

Grunig, J., and Hunt, T. (1984) *Managing Public Relations*, London: Holt, Rinehart and Winston.

Herman and Chomsky, N. (1998) *Manufacturing Consent*. New York: Pantheon.

Heywood, A. (1997) *Politics*. Basingstoke: Macmillan.

Jackson, N. and Lilleker, D. (2004) 'Politicians in the press, on the web, and in your face: an attempt at interaction of just public relations?', *European Journal of Communication*, 19 (4): 427–554.

Johnston, R.J. (1987) *Money and Votes: Spending and Election Results*. London: Croom Helm.

Laswell, H.H. (1927) *Propaganda Techniques in the World War.* New York: Knopf.

Lees, C. (2005) 'Political marketing in Germany', in D.G. Lilleker and J. Lees-Marshment, *Political Marketing in Comparative Perspective*. Manchester: Manchester University Press.

Lees-Marshment, J. and Lilleker, D.G. (2005) 'Introduction: rethinking political party behaviour', in D.G. Lilleker and J. Lees-Marshment *Political Marketing: A Comparative Perspective*. Manchester: Manchester University Press.

McNair, B. (2003) *An Introduction to Political Communication*. London: Routledge.

Mancini, P. (1999) 'New frontiers in political professionalism', *Political Communication*, 16: 231–45.

Marshall, P.D. (1997) *Celebrity and Power: Fame in Contemporary Culture*. London: University of Minnesota Press.

Mikardo, I. (1988) *Backbencher*. London: Weidenfeld & Nicolson.

Moloney, K. (2001) 'The rise and fall of spin: Changes of fashion in the presentation of UK politics', *Journal of Public Affairs*, 1 (2): 124–35.

Moon, N. (1999) *Opinion Polls: History Theory and Practice*. Manchester: Manchester University Press.

Negrine, R. and Lilleker, D. (2003) 'The professionalisation of media-based campaigning in Britain 1966–2001: The rise of a proactive media strategy', *Journalism Studies*, 4 (2): 199–212.

Norris, P. (2000) *A Virtuous Circle: Political Communications in Postindustrial Societies*. Cambridge: Cambridge University Press

Pels, D. (2003) 'Aesthetic representation and political style', in J. Corner and D. Pels, *Media and the Restyling of Politics*. London: Sage.

Reeves, R. (1997) 'The question of media bias', in S. Iyengar and R. Reeves, *Do the Media Govern? Politicians, Voters and Reporters in America*. London: Sage.

Rodgers, J. (2004) *Spatializing International Politics: Analysing Activism on the Internet*. London: Routledge.

Said, E. (2000) 'Apocalypse now', *Index on Censorship*, 5: 49–53.

Scammell, M. (1995) *Designer Politics*. London: Macmillan.

Schlesinger, P. (1987) *Putting Reality Together*. London: Methuen.

Street, J. (1997) *Politics and Popular Culture*. Cambridge: Polity.

Street, J. (2001) *Mass Media, Politics and Democracy*. Basingstoke: Palgrave Macmillan.

Wring, D. (2001) 'The 'Tony' press: Media coverage of the election campaign', in A.P. Geddes and J. Tonge, *Labour's Second Landslide: The British General Election 2001*. Manchester: Manchester University Press.

political
communication

19

How to use this book

The research texts all introduce a range of concepts, some of which are unique to political communication; others are borrowed from other disciplines. Concepts are ways of thinking; they are the elements that link together a range of ideas and their practical applications. However, concepts are abstract; they are universally applicable and can often be used in different ways depending on the subject being studied. This book seeks to help newcomers to the subject of political communication to understand further the key concepts that relate to this challenging area. Although each entry is in the form of a discrete essay, the intention is for a dual function. First, it can be read as a textbook to provide an introduction to political communication in all its forms. Secondly, and possibly after a full reading, it can be used as a reminder or aide-memoire, of a term's meaning and practical application. Each term is introduced by a brief definition that will be sufficient to grasp the simple meaning and uses of the concept. This is followed by a format that, first of all, establishes the origins of the term, either in academic writing or practical politics and how it links to the other concepts in the volume, each being highlighted in bold within the text to facilitate cross-referencing. Secondly, the key features of the concept are described by providing practical examples from the real world, using a range of political systems both current and historical. Thirdly, the discussion is brought up to date by introducing the most current thinking, providing a balanced argument for why the concept's practical dimension can be viewed as positive or negative and introducing the key authors. A final section offers suggestions for further reading.

Each entry should enable the reader to think about the concepts, to understand them theoretically and practically and then expand upon the discussion by applying them to current affairs. Many of the examples used here could be out of date to you the reader. You should seek your own examples, from the current affairs happening around you. You should be reading the newspapers and watching television and when doing so identify the political communication, its source, the way in which the media use it, and how it may be received, and then consider which concepts apply to it. The purpose of this book is to act as a foundation for this.

Key Concepts in
Political Communication

Aestheticisation

Aestheticisation relates to the fact that political communication has become increasingly more about style and presentation, and increasingly influenced by popular culture, in an attempt to become more modern-looking, relevant and in touch with society.

ORIGINS AND LINKS

It was German sociologist Ulrich Beck (1994) who noted societies' increasing obsession with appearance rather than substance; that the style in which one dresses, the care over appearance, the image and presentation can be as important to the **audience** when processing a political message as what is actually said or done. While Beck related this phenomenon largely to popular music and television, others, such as Frank Ankersmit, Dick Pels and John Street, the latter in the context of **popular culture**, have presented evidence that politicians are also looking at the aesthetics of their image communication as well as, or often prior to, the substance.

Aestheticisation can also be linked to **emotionalisation**, what some prefer to call feminisation and the reduction of a macho-style of communication, and sometimes **authenticity**, all of which can encourage a greater connection with the political class and lead to greater trust. It promotes **style** and **packaging**, is a feature of much **political advertising** and **rhetoric** and has been accused of being evidence of the **dumbing down** and **mediatisation** of political communication and indeed political activity in general.

KEY FEATURES

The recent personalisation of politics, and the transformation of some politicians into celebrities with media interest focusing as much on their lifestyles as their policies, could be classified under aestheticisation. However, this would be to misuse the term. According to Ankersmit (1994), for a politician to project an aesthetic quality it is not enough to appear the same as the people – so reflecting those they represent. Instead, he argues that political actors should represent an ideal of the

political communication

society or ideal self of the audience member. Thus the leader, or would-be leader, should project an image that is aesthetically better, that which we aspire to rather than that which we are. Therefore it is not enough to appear to have sartorial elegance, as many argue is the case with flamboyant politicians, such as the late Dutch independent populist Pim Fortuyn. The politician must also exhibit a moral countenance, as was attempted by the UK Conservative government under John Major when he discussed re-adopting Victorian moral values of the family and society. Pels argues that this is largely a preserve of right-wing populists, such as Austria's Jorge Haider, who rhetorically discuss a 'better' society while projecting a modernist image. However, parallels between Haider and UK Prime Minister Tony Blair suggest that this is not solely a trait linked with fascistic leaders. The latter came to power on his modernist outlook, his reduced distance from the public through appropriate uses of formality and informality, and his 'feminine' style of exhibiting emotions – particularly in his speech following the death of Princess Diana on 31 August 1997 when he managed to encapsulate the public mood with the phrase 'the people's princess'.

THE ACADEMIC AND PRACTICAL DEBATES

The key issue here surrounds authenticity. It is claimed that Tony Blair is an accomplished actor, and as such is able to project a false persona. Haider and Fortuyn, on the other hand, were both revealed to be projecting an image of society that contrasted sharply with their ability to create such a society, not to mention with their personal behaviour. Therefore, we often find aestheticisation viewed as a rhetorical device as empty as Fortuyn's claim, despite his millionaire status and homosexuality, to 'embody the true soul of the Dutch people' (Pels, 2003: 60).

However, those who promote the requirement to bring more aesthetic representation into politics argue it is essential to separate politics from being viewed as a game played out by managers. Actually, when thinking of politics and leadership, people need something to believe in. These can be ideas, ideologies, values or morals, but they also need a physical representation. Often it is a gap in society that can be filled by leaders with a semi-fascistic style, simply because no other political actor is able, or considers it necessary, to offer aesthetic leadership instead of managerialism. However, the aesthetic image that is presented must have substance, it must be believable and demonstrated through action as well as style and cannot be just symbolic or rhetorical. If the image is nothing more than a rhetorical device the public will decode it as just another part of the game of political competition.

FURTHER READING

On the aestheticisation of society see Ulrich Beck (1994) 'The debate on the 'individualization theory' in today's sociology in Germany', *Sociologie*, 3: 191–200. The aestheticisation of politics is covered in more depth in Frank Ankersmit (1994) *Aesthetic Politics: Political Philosophy Beyond Fact and Value*. Stanford: Stanford University Press; Dick Pels (2003) 'Aesthetic representation and political style: Rebalancing identity and difference in media democracy', in J. Corner and D. Pels, *Media and the Restyling of Politics*. London: Sage.

Agenda-Setting

In a mediated democracy, politicians often battle to determine what is on the front page of the newspapers, or the leading item on the news. The agenda is the news of a particular day, more specifically the story, and how the news is told. Not only do politicians battle with each other, they also battle with the media, who may have opposing news values and wish to treat a story differently to that which the politician desires.

ORIGINS AND LINKS

The concept of agenda-setting is founded in the study of the media, and particularly the press, and is linked to the famous adage that the media 'cannot tell you what to think, only what to think about' (McCombs and Shaw, 1972). The agenda is, at the simplest level, what is the news; at a more sophisticated level, how that news is reported. A key function of political communication is to make the public think about an issue in a way that is favourable to the sender of the message. This means that every organisation that desires to influence the public politically must attempt to control what ideas become dominant in the public sphere. So, environmentalist groups will try to, firstly, get their stories into the news and, secondly, control the way they that those stories are received by media audiences. This may well put them into conflict with political parties, corporations and other groups in society; each of whom will wish to set the news agenda. In a thriving pluralist democracy all voices should be heard; however, the ability of some groups to dominate the agenda can restrict pluralism.

Agenda-setting is the important part of any **campaign**, but can have a negative impact on **civic society** and the **public sphere** due to the public becoming **cynical** about the information it receives. Political parties may operate on **information subsidies**, which can restrict public access to the facts and enforce the notion of the **hegemonic model** in an information society. However, agenda-setting plays a key role in any political organisation's **news management** strategy, it provides work for **spin-doctors** and is a key feature of the **public relations state**.

KEY FEATURES

Organisations which aim to strategically set and control the news agenda will employ communication officers, the spin-doctors, who will attempt to control the information available to the media to ensure a negative line cannot be taken. While this has become a dominant feature of US and UK political campaigning, this is not an Anglo-American phenomenon, it is a feature of every pluralist democracy: though some organisations are more overt in their tactics than others. The philosophy equally underpins policies that seek to control the media, as in many countries in eastern Europe. The problem with identifying agenda-setting is that it is only seen by the politician and the journalist, and although we may find indications in hindsight, or hear accounts of the practice, it is hard to detect in real time; thus the public are argued to be susceptible to the subtle controls over the news they receive.

THE ACADEMIC AND PRACTICAL DEBATES

In a pluralist democracy, where there are a number of competing voices on any issue, it seems obvious that all of these will also compete over the media agenda. It is the main form of communication with a mass audience, and so a key mode of influencing the public. That is accepted as a norm. However, there are greater debates over the extent to which each actor competes on a level playing field. Pressure groups can find themselves excluded from the agenda (see the research of Anders

Hansen), while others suspect that corporations pay for greater control (Naom Chomsky and Gerald Sussman often relate to these notions in studies of US politics). It has long been noted that there are insider and outsider groups in any society, and that the insider groups have far greater access to the news agenda than those outside. While there is no identifiable community of the powerful, we still hear that the agenda is set by certain groups: newspaper editors or media moguls; politicians and their corporate allies; the military–industrial complex. What these works agree on is that the lack of open access stifles debate, it increases public cynicism if they do not agree that the news is all-encompassing, yet they are unable to do anything about it because they lack full, open access to objective, balanced arguments. While access to the agenda can mobilise, for example environmentalists, lack of access demobilises those who need persuading into political action. Thus it creates a civic society that is repressed politically, that feels it is impotent, and so ignores its political duty pursuing consumerist rather than political power.

However, many posit that it is the media that set the agenda, and that each media organisation has its own agenda; therefore the political communicators are compelled to respond with news management techniques. The parameters of the media agenda can often depend far more on a newspaper's readership or a news programme's audience, and will not bow to government or corporate communication strategies. It is the editor who decides what makes news, and how this should be reported, and so political communicators have little real power beyond the subsidisation of information from within their organisation. Because political actors need media coverage, they have to play the media's game. This may not increase the access to information, but it restricts the power of the propagandist over the public sphere. Such debates are often about apportioning blame, sometimes upon the public for relying on single, biased, sources for their information; however, most agree that agenda-setting restricts access to information and on that premise alone argue the practice is damaging to the principle of democratic pluralism.

FURTHER READING

An introduction can be found in M.E. McCombs and D.L. Shaw (1972) 'The agenda-setting function of the press', *Public Opinion Quarterly*, 36, 176–87; or D.L. Shaw and M.E. McCombs (1977) *The Emergence of American Political Issues: The Agenda-Setting Function of the Press*. New York: St Paul Press. More recent work has moved to a dual focus on both the media and the political organisations, for which, see J.W. Dearing and

E.M. Rogers (1996) *Agenda-Setting*. (Thousand Oaks, CA: Sage); T.A. Birkland (1998) *After Disaster: Agenda Setting, Public Policy and Focusing Events*. Washington, DC: Georgetown University Press). On the responses by political parties see H. Semetko, J.G. Blumler, M. Gurevitch and D. Weaver (1991) *The Formation of Campaign Agendas: A Comparative Analysis of Party and Media Roles in Recent American and British Elections*. Hillsdale, NJ: Lawrence Erlbaum).

Americanisation/ Professionalisation

Explanations of the way in which political communication has become better, or more strategic, often talk about the way in which it has become more professional or been professionalised. This is used as a blanket term to describe the way it is better, or appears to be less amateurish, than in the past. While there are a number of reasons for the evolution of political communication, the rise of more efficient and demanding means of communication as well as the decline of voter partisanship (dealignment), some also discuss professionalisation in terms of Americanisation. This means that in response to technological and societal developments, politicians in the broader Americas, western and eastern Europe, parts of Asia and Australasia have borrowed ideas, techniques and in some cases personnel working in political communication in the USA to improve their campaigning or governmental communication. While the two terms are not of the same meaning, they are often treated as synonymous and there is significant overlap in the way that academic studies introduce them both.

ORIGINS AND LINKS

The most influential accounts of the evolution of political communication, though centred largely upon **campaigning**, the most vigorous aspect of the process, are provided, firstly, by Jay Blumler and Dennis Kavanagh and, slightly more recently, by Pippa Norris. While they do not map onto one another exactly, both see changes occurring, firstly, in the 1960s and then again in the 1990s. In the period up to the 1960s, Norris's pre-modern era, the party was firmly in control of communication conveying its message more at the local level, in public meetings, than via the mass media. Blumler and Kavanagh argue that television shifted control away from parties as well as shifting communication away from the local, interpersonal level. Norris also highlights that the **dealignment** process led parties to concentrate more on national coordination and using a greater level of selling within campaign communication. The current era, what Norris refers to as that of the postmodern campaign, sees a larger amount of diversity in terms of the levels at which communication is conducted, due to a greater focus on individually tailored marketing communication (**narrowcasting**), greater use of **advertising**, and **permanent campaigning**.

The Americanisation thesis dovetails neatly with this, as many of the techniques that Norris associates with postmodern campaigning, and Blumler and Kavanagh with the Third Age, have been employed previously by US political parties and organisations. Analysts of political communication claim that strategies that are deemed successful in the US are carefully observed by actors across the democratic world then copied, often with the support of campaign consultants imported from the US. In fact, many link it to the process of **globalisation**. It is argued that this has altered the style of political communication and we therefore hear reference to designer politics and packaging as well as increased use of **negativity** in **advertising**. It is hotly contested, however, the extent to which Americanisation is actually taking place, not to mention whether the result of such cross-cultural borrowing is positive or not.

What commentators tend to agree on is that the driving force behind the process of professionalisation is a combination of the social and political change stemming from **dealignment** and the rise of **consumerism**, and the increasing market-orientation of the media from information provider to entertainer. These have led parties to rethink their strategies, often as a result of electoral failure. However, the changes implemented have also impacted on party behaviour by accelerating the professionalisation process, leading to the use of **political marketing** and its emphasis in communication of **style** over substance. This process is illustrated in Figure 4.

political
communication

31

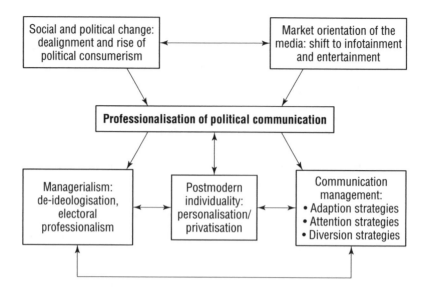

Figure 4   *The process of professionalisation (adapted from Holtz-Bacha, 2002)*

KEY FEATURES

Key to the postmodern era, or Third Age, where an Americanised model of campaigning is commonplace are:

- *Nationally coordinated campaigns which are operationalised in a decentralised, local contest.* We therefore find national policies translated into a local context. This requires, however, a strong local organisation, lack of which hindered the Austrian parties' campaigns in 1999; on the other hand both candidates in the US 2004 presidential election enjoyed strong local support and were thus able to develop a consistent and successful campaign at the state level.
- *The creation of campaign units within parties and the use of consultants.* In preparation for the 2001 Danish general election, both the Social Democratic Party and the Liberal Party hired professional consultants and created communication departments similar to those introduced by Blair in the UK and Clinton in the USA (Mair et al., 2004: 221–4).
- *The use of market intelligence.* Various aspects of party behaviour, image and policies can be designed through market intelligence. The UK's New Labour 1997 manifesto pledges, the modernisation of Germany's SPD between 1998 and 2002 and the identification of the

needs of target groups by Italy's National Alliance and Christian Democrats were all designed using opinion polls and focus groups.

- *Communication focused on the media.* Favourable reportage becomes all important and the needs of media organisations become paramount in the design of messages. This links to **spin**, particularly in the case of the UK's New Labour government.
- *Narrowcasting* (see concept, pp. 46–8).
- *The permanent campaign* (see concept, pp. 143–7).

These features link well to a further thesis, McDonaldisation. George Ritzer (1993, 1998) argued that society, and so politics and its communication, had adapted to a model of organisation that was similar to that of the global fast food restaurant. He identified four key features: that they had become more efficient in their delivery, with a greater focus on the receiver; that quantity was prioritised over quality, linking to the repeat–remind of **soundbites** to transmit core **messages**; that campaigns were predictable in their standard and techniques; and that control was centralised, so all local branches reiterated the parties symbolism and slogans.

While these features are becoming increasingly perceived as part of the globalisation of political communication methods, usually mirroring developments in the US, many do not accept that professionalisation equates to Americanisation. In fact, many comparative analysts argue that professionalisation has a far more nationally contextualised character than the Americanisation thesis allows.

THE ACADEMIC AND PRACTICAL DEBATES

If, firstly, we look at the terminology, both are criticised for obscuring as much as they explain. Professionalisation can be used in two ways: one suggests a career with rules, codes of behaviour and relative permanence; the second suggests non-amateur in appearance. While some do discuss the rise of the professional politician, and importantly the professional political consultant, few suggest the latter as being any more than a hobby alongside a career in public relations, lobbying or strategic communications. It is the latter definition, one which is rather vague and nebulous, that is applied to political communication. While commentators agree on the above key features, they use professionalisation to describe political organisations and their communications strategy, the employment of consultants and their skills, as well as the style, modes and targeting of communication. These differing uses, together with the discussion of ages and eras, do not allow us to understand when professionalisation took place, the cause, or who instituted the change (Lilleker and Negrine, 2002). An evolutionary perspective would suggest change is constant, and that each political communicator appeared professional within their own era, as did their style and modes. Alternatively, can we identify a single event, or series of events, that have caused clearly quantifiable, immediate changes? Few do suggest this, so are we actually seeing an evolved style that appears more professional now but that in the future will appear amateurish? This is a question which must be considered when looking at literature suggesting all is professional.

A similar argument can be made over the use of Americanisation to explain one key cause and designer of the professional era. Swanson and Mancini (1996: 4) offer the thesis not as a conclusion, but as a reference point. Blumler and Kavanagh note the significant similarities in style of the US and UK campaigns post-1992; however, it is argued that this is due to some, key similarities in the political systems: the two-party competition and winner takes all elections being the most important. This appears to have driven much UK–US comparative analysis, but causes similar approaches to flounder when applied to differing systems. Holtz-Bacha et al. (1994) compared advertising in the UK, US and Germany during the early 1990s and found that while negativity was a feature of two systems, the tradition of coalition governments in Germany made such techniques totally inappropriate. Similar differences were evidenced in a global comparative study of political marketing where Germany, again, was seen as distinct in character (Lilleker and Lees-Marshment, 2005). Chapters in Mair et al. (2004) also highlight the problems with Americanising campaigning in France, Denmark and Spain. Thus critics like Holtz-Bacha argue that any study of Americanisation must focus as much on the differences as the similarities before coming to a conclusion that all nations are operating on an American model in the current era.

Critics would also highlight the inappropriateness of adopting American techniques. While the cost may be prohibitive anyway, the use of negativity in campaign communications can alienate supporters and has been blamed on the collapse of public confidence in political parties in the US, the UK, Germany and Scandinavia; thus even those countries that borrow some aspects, not all, from the postmodern model, can reap negative political consequences. This was highlighted particularly in the Holtz-Bacha et al. comparative study involving Germany.

Therefore much debate circulates around the use of the terms themselves as well as the effects of the contingent techniques. However, many do identify that the techniques associated with the postmodern era are becoming far more widespread, therefore it is appropriate to talk of both professionalisation and Americanisation provided one is aware of their limits as explanatory terms as well as their inappropriateness for responding to societal changes and technological advancements in all political systems.

FURTHER READING

For the 'ages' of political communication and campaigning see Jay Blumler and Dennis Kavanagh (1999) 'The Third Age of political communication: Influences and Features', *Political Communication*, 16: 209–30; Pippa Norris (2000) 'The evolution of campaign communications', in *A Virtuous Circle: Political Communications in Postindustrial Societies*. Cambridge: Cambridge University Press. pp. 137–62. The key features of the Third Age or postmodern campaign era are described in both works. The Americanisation thesis is introduced in D.L. Swanson and P. Mancini (1996) *Politics, Media and Modern Democracy: An International Study of Innovations in Electoral Campaigning and Their Consequences*. Westport, CT: Praeger. It is further debated within R. Negrine and S. Papathanassopoulos (1996) 'The "Americanisation" of political communication', *Harvard International Journal of Press/Politics*, 1 (2): 45–62. For a debate on professionalisation as an explanative term see D.G. Lilleker and R. Negrine (2002) 'Professionalisation: Of what? Since when? By whom?', *Harvard International Journal of Press/Politics*, 7 (4): 98–103. Good comparative studies of Americanisation, and its limits, are C. Holtz-Bacha, L.L. Kaid and A. Johnston (1994) 'Political television advertising in Western democracies: A comparison of campaign broadcasts in the United States, Germany and France, *Political Communication*, 11: 67–80; for a similar view of professionalisation see Christina Holtz-Bacha (2002) 'Professionalization of political communication: The case of the 1998 SPD campaign', *Journal of Political Marketing*, 1 (4): 23–37. For McDonaldisation see George Ritzer (1993) *The McDonaldization of Society*. London: Sage; George Ritzer (1998) *The McDonaldization Thesis*. London: Sage.

35

Audiences

The term audience is used to describe a number of largely unidentifiable people, all of whom will be using a particular media or receiving a particular message. Audiences are often treated as homogenous and so are constructions of the imagination of the message sender only. Thus we talk of their being multiple, infinite audiences, each belonging to a particular communicator or message. Message originators often view audiences as passive; however, this would be erroneous.

ORIGINS AND LINKS

Audience research emerged from the study of media effects, therefore such concepts are seldom related to political communication apart from as a mediating force. This is an oversight that is currently being addressed. An understanding of audiences is very important, as it is audience members who ultimately decide whether to accept the message or not, and who are able to relay political messages within the **public sphere** that can influence group political decisions within any social community (families, workplace, friends), so blocking out many of the effects the media are credited with (Lenart, 1994; Graber, 2001).

The audience is introduced into political science as the **public sphere**. Through debates surrounding this theoretical construct, we find discussions surrounding the extent to which it is the elite or the public that create policy. Some argue that the power possessed by audience members mean that it is the latter situation that predominates. This is described by some scholars as an audience democracy (Manin, 1997), and is synonymous with the notion of a market-oriented government (see **political marketing**, pp. 00–00). However, political communication is always designed with the audience in mind, the use of marketing tools, **aestheticisation** and **emotionalisation** is intended to have greater appeal, or relevance, to the audience. While it can be described as, and often is just **spin** or **propaganda**, its aim is to mobilise the audience/electorate, encourage them to participate, though in the way required by the communicator, and engage with political activity.

KEY FEATURES

Audiences, as already noted, are an artificial construct: the term used by Philip Schlesinger was 'imagined community'. The constructions aid media organisations, researchers and regulators, as well as political organisations that use the media, to target groups in society effectively to ensure they are reached, that they receive information of interest to them and, ultimately, feel fulfilled as participants in the democratic process. Each media outlet has an imagined audience; daytime television focuses on a predominantly female audience of housewives, tabloid newspapers on those with a lower interest in 'hard news' and who seek entertainment, or soft news (**infotainment**). Thus political organisations try to place their communication into the correct outlet to reach the key audiences, **messages** are constructed that are relevant to that audience and use symbolism and language that they can understand and respond to.

However, the postmodern audience is no longer as easy to identify as was the case previously. They are argued to be more sophisticated, they are not homogenous and have multiple identities, thus the housewife may have greater interests than are catered for in daytime television schedules and may not identify with the symbols used in the advertising that is contiguous to 'their' programmes. It is argued that the postmodern audience member decodes every message according to their own individual identities, which are often hidden beneath the more obvious characteristics that the communicator has used as a homogenising factor when constructing their audience.

Politicians have a greater problem in reaching the postmodern audience. While a product that is advertised may be viewed as relevant, the political product is less tangible, more difficult to communicate in a way that is relevant to the whole of their electorate and so they can find that they have difficulty entering the **public sphere**. Thus tactics such as **aestheticisation** and **emotionalisation** can be used, as well as more blunt instruments such as **spin** with its public relations philosophy of repeat–remind. They also try to strategically **segment** the audience, in the same way as marketers do, though this can be problematic.

THE ACADEMIC AND PRACTICAL DEBATES

Current debates focus on the link between audience decoding of messages and voting behaviour. While it continues to be true that predisposition towards a party, organisation or ideology means messages that fit those predispositions are more readily accepted, the number of voters with party predispositions is ever decreasing. Ideology is more individualistically defined, and the postmodern voter selects from a range of causes, ideas and ideals not thinking of themselves as being on the traditional left–right political spectrum. This complexity means that voters are harder to reach and thus, perhaps, more easy to estrange.

Complex models have been developed to explain voter behaviour, each of which aid communicators. Anthony Downs (1957) presented one theory, one since updated (Heath et al., 2001), to explain how the voter makes a personal calculation of which party to support on the basis of which party will be best for them personally. Others promote rational choice theories (Popkin, 1991), where we try to assess who is best for everyone. Yet we still find there are emotional models, where voters acquire an attachment to key aspects of a party, such as image, radicalism, populism or other less rational aspects of the party political product. It is the latter that have been argued to be the root of the support for Austria's neo-Nazi Jorge Haider and Holland's right-wing populist Pim Fortuyn. But how does this help us to understand the audience?

The simple answer is that it does not. Logically we all have individualistic, rational and emotional selves, each competing to inform our behaviour. What occurs in audience members' minds when they receive any piece of communication, or indeed when they later go into the ballot box, is unknown to us. Experiments into the use of **negativity**, and the importance of interpersonal communication (Lenart, 1994; Grabert, 2001) go some way, but experiments are unnatural, thus we still know little of how the audience works 'in the wild, uncontrollable environment' of their own homes and lives.

FURTHER READING

Audience research from a media perspective is introduced in J. Hartley (1992) *The Politics of Pictures: The Creation of the Public in the Age of Popular Media*. London: Routledge. A classic text, which touches on politics broadly, remains Philip Schlesinger (1991) *Media, State and Nation: Political Violence and Collective Identities*. London: Sage. On audience democracy see: B. Manin (1997) *The Principles of Representative Government*. Cambridge: Cambridge University Press. For political audience research see D. Graber (2001) *Processing Politics: Learning from Television in the Internet Age*. Chicago: University of Chicago Press; S. Lenart (1994) *Shaping Political Attitudes: The Impact of Interpersonal Communication and Mass Media*. London: Sage; S. Popkin (1991) *The Reasoning Voter*. Chicago: University of Chicago Press. A synthesis of debates on voting behaviour can be found in A.F. Heath, R.M. Jowell and J.K. Curtice (2001) *The Rise of New Labour: Party Policies and Voter Choices.* Oxford: Oxford University Press; See also Anthony Downs (1957) *An Economic Theory of Voting.* New York: Harper & Row.

Authenticity

> **The perception of political actors as being 'real people', intrinsically a part of the community they represent, rather than being detached and part of an elite.**

ORIGINS AND LINKS

Politicians of previous generations were likely to be the better educated, wealthier, not to mention older and male, section of society. They were an elite who were better equipped to govern society than the ill-informed masses, matching, to some extent, Plato's notion of the ideal society. Slowly the desire of society to be run by such a political cadre has been eroded. While qualities such as education, wisdom or reliability may still be necessary for electoral success, the concept of trust, while always important, has taken on new meanings as well as being measured differently. The public are able to look into the lives of politicians with greater scrutiny, helped by an intrusive, investigative media. They demand that political actors are representative, that they are a member of the community in a Wittgensteinian sense, meaning that the identity of political actors is recognised as partially representing our perception of ourselves. The identity may be diffused across a range of actors, all of whom may or may not be members of one party, and be constructed by the **audience**. This means that authenticity, being perceived as a real person that is recognised as a part of the community, is largely perceptual and is thus difficult to construct by the actor.

It is argued by John Street (1997) and Dick Pels (2004) that it is celebrities that actually do possess authenticity, that they are seen, despite their rich lifestyles, as being 'just like us'. Footballers, like David Beckham or Pele, musicians, such as Robbie Williams and Bono, or actors, like Jude

political communication

39

Law, seem to possess a down-to-earth quality that means global audiences identify with them. Politicians desire a similar quality, which some, like US President Bill Clinton seemed to have naturally, and so try to transmit a stylised image. This leads to discussion of designer or **celebrity politics**, **aestheticisation**, **packaging** and the **dumbing down** of political discussion.

KEY FEATURES

A prime example of an expression of authenticity is the appearance of political actors in non-political contexts. Thus we see this reflected in the use of chat shows by Bill Clinton, Tony Blair and a range of global political figures; appearances at concerts by US presidential candidate John Kerry and Russian President Boris Yeltsin; and attempts to link to celebrities: in 2004 Bono spoke at the UK's Labour Party Conference. He was neither on message, nor supportive, but clearly it was his kudos that was sought, not his politics.

Politicians seeking to develop an authentic image will present themselves as being more emotional, and allow their private lives to be publicised; though perhaps with strict controls over information. They will balance their television appearances between serious political debate and more populist programmes. They will also try to be seen in 'real' contexts and with the 'right people'; to some this would be celebrities to borrow positive connotations, in other cases it would be connecting with the public.

THE ACADEMIC AND PRACTICAL DEBATES

There are two issues relating to the application of authenticity. First, and as Pels (2004) notes, the quality of appearing real is not decided by that individual but by the audience and by the media. While Tony Blair enjoyed much positive media from the time he became party leader in 1994 to around the time of his party's second year in government 1998–99, there followed a period of marked contrast. Once sought as a guest for singer and chat show host Des O'Connor and comedian Frank Skinner, it became increasingly rare to see Blair in such contexts. Possibly the invitations were rare, or it was perceived that the public no longer accepted the image as authentic but were convinced that it was manufactured. Thus the authenticity must be believed to be real and not fake, and if the media does turn against a political actor and highlight instances of spin, lying or generally 'faking', the authenticity is gone. A lack of access to the non-political programming means that an image of authenticity cannot be promoted and so public perception is limited to media framing.

A further issue, discussed widely in relation to the emotionalisation, packaging and marketing of politics, is that this is not really what politics should be about. That the focus upon the aesthetic, image-related, and peripheral detracts from the serious business of policy. Some would argue that this is because it is the area where postmodern politicians are either strongest or weakest thus, like Austria's populist neo-fascist Jorge Haider, image is either peripheral or becomes everything.

Therefore, although it is argued that audiences need to connect with politicians, this is a difficult process to manage due to the limited access to the media and limited control over subsequent reportage, and it may be damaging to political debate in the long-term as politics becomes reduced to another aspect of our diet of popular culture.

FURTHER READING

On politics and popular culture see John Street (1997) *Politics and Popular Culture*. Cambridge: Polity Press. Various chapters in J. Corner and D. Pels (2003) *Media and the Restyling of Politics*. London: Sage deal with similar issues, particular those by Dick Pels, John Street, Lisbet Van Zoonen and W. Lance Bennet.

Brands/Branding

political communication

41

> *A brand is a symbolic entity, it is a name and logo used to identify a manufacturer or service provider that is instantly recognisable within a market-place; leading out of this, the process of branding is the development of the logo, symbols and names and ensures that which it stands for is recognised within the market.*

As noted in the above definition, brands and branding are associated with the marketing of manufacturers of goods or providers of a service. Most people in the UK would recognise banks such as Barclays, as would the Dutch recognise Abn-Amro and the French the BNP (Banque Nationale Paris), and globally there are McDonalds, Coca-Cola, Fosters, Budweiser, Shell: a whole host of recognisable brands. While their recognition may well suggest they can be trusted; more important for a brand is the building of something called equity. Equity represents a range of qualities that the public recognise to be synonymous with the brand and that leads them to be trusted, it may be reliability for banks, for McDonalds it could be cheap, honest, quick food. There may also be national symbols attached to brands or brands may even attach themselves to a political ideology or cause. Whatever they do affects the brands equity among sections of its market. Equity can be earned and lost, and it is used in times of crisis to reduce loss of trust and militate against negative media coverage. Some refer to equity as being like savings; it is built up through positive interactions over time and reduces the potency of the few negative interactions.

Recent studies have linked the concept of branding to political parties, and perhaps it is easy to see why. Like any other organisation parties employ logos and symbols to define themselves; the UK Conservative Party use the 'Torch of Freedom' while Labour uses a rose. Equally parties possess equity, usually based on their competence in office, but also linked to public perception of their policies, key spokespersons or even their representatives at the local level. Most important, however, is that parties usually have a clear **ideology**, the voters know what it is that they represent. This can be linked purely to a position on the left–right spectrum, but usually has more to do with some other political platform, such as the representation of a segment of society. It is argued that this is particularly important in nations where there are multiple parties within the parliament; Sweden, for example, has seven parties vying for power, each maintaining clear political distance from their opponents. In contrast, in nations where there are few parties, like the USA and UK, a clear brand identity may not be as important, as there is always latitude for movement.

While branding has been introduced as interest in **political marketing** has grown, it is not a new concept. However, the increased uses of branding techniques is clearly an element of the **professionalisation** of party campaigning and can be linked to the post-dealignment use of voter **segmentation** and **narrowcasting** and is caused by the **consumerisation** of electoral behaviour.

KEY FEATURES

While branding may be argued to be antithetical to political party behaviour, the features of a party and that of a brand are not markedly dissimilar, nor does any aspect of branding behaviour lead to contradictions in what could be recognised as traditional party behaviour. At the heart of any brand is the kernel, which contains the ethos, ideology and beliefs of the brand. While for corporate organisations the kernel may represent nothing more than a drive for profit, this is not always the case; many companies are founded around actively protecting the environment. The ethos of a company will be set by shareholders or the founders, as is the case with most parties; it is the founders and original members that will write the constitutions and gather like-minded individuals to promote the ideas they share. Surrounding the brand's kernel are the codes; these would be enshrined in a constitution or mission statement. Codes would act as constraints upon political policy, party or organisation behaviour, and the messages created to give the brand external character.

Externally the brand values are communicated through the name, which can be symbolic to a party's members as well as voters: such as the use of the epithets 'Christian', 'National' or 'Socialist'. The logo will also represent that which the party stands for; thus while the symbol of a dove or doves is used to denote peace, and symbols of other birds to denote freedom, still other symbols can be used to signify an attachment to workers. The organisation's messages and behaviour are perhaps the most important signifier of what the brand stands for; perceptions are built over a long period of time. Therefore any changes to brands must be gradual and evolutionary, if not, attachments will weaken and trust will be lost: this has certainly been the case for New Labour in the UK.

Brands will also identify segments in society with whom they build a relationship. These are often loose relationships in countries with a few mass parties; however, in nations with many parties, voter segments must be identified clearly and parties try not to impinge on one another's core segment as this will impair future working relations if there is an opportunity for power-sharing. An example of segmentation can be offered by a review of Finnish political parties, where it is common for there to be three or four parties sharing power in a coalition government: Table 1 shows the major parties and their voter segments.

What we see here are parties delineating the electorate on a number of different lines: there are social demographics, affluence and attitude to aspiration, membership of a national group, religious beliefs and political

Table 1 *Party segmentation in Finland*

Finnish Social Democratic Party (SSDP)	Solidly working class, blue-collar workers in heavy industry. Left-of-centre politics of collectivism and state intervention
Finnish Centre Party (KESK)	Affluent working class, small business owners. Centre politics, mixed economy, traditional values
National Coalition Party (KOK)	The old, traditionalist, pro-Scandinavians. Right-of-centre, strong state nationalism with free enterprise economics
Swedish People's Party (SFP)	Swedish-speaking elites. Minority rights, mixture of state intervention and free economy
Finnish Christian Democrats (KD)	Christians believing in moral government, openness, morality and Christian values

beliefs. Other, smaller, parties, like the Communists, also fit around them, but are usually excluded from power. Currently the SSDP and KESK hold power, with the KOK marginalized for the first time in 16 years; the result, it is argued, of their segment's decline in recent years. Their problem has been that the party cannot be easily rebranded, while they are unable to encroach on their competitor's segments.

THE ACADEMIC AND PRACTICAL DEBATES

Branding is not a term used that often, though studies in political marketing have increased its deployment. It is, however, a useful lens through which to view the behaviour of political parties. The debates centre on the notion of branding and rebranding, particularly in light of the successes and failures of these strategies in the US and UK. While branding can be argued to be the cause of voters moving away from a party, or more commonly the loss of core supporters or members, this is a misrepresentation of branding. Few corporate organisations are able to rebrand themselves overnight, or even over long periods, and they do not face the glare of the media spotlight in the same way as political parties do. Therefore it is important to recognise the importance of brand symbols and ethos within politics and the fact that all communication must not contradict the kernel and codes of the brand. This is where parties appear to face the most problems.

As the Finnish right-of-centre parties saw their support base crumble, the only available tactic that could be employed to attempt to regain support was to encourage Marjo Matikainen-Kallstrom, former gold medal winning Olympic skier, to stand for the party leadership. This represents an example of a party trying to build positive brand associations through the creation of a strong link to a celebrity. In contrast, in the US the 'New' Democrats and in the UK 'New' Labour, attempted the same through strategies aimed at distancing themselves from their own history and projecting a modern, new, radical and different image. While this was successful to a point, and was helped considerably by the charismatic, media-friendly young leaders Clinton and Blair, in the case of New Labour, support among 'core voters' declined. This was particularly the case when the party proposed policies that voters thought were counter to their perception of what the party represented. While the party had been rebranded to fit with the template provided through qualitative research with weak Conservative voters, the core voters were not consulted; this left the party with a weaker activist base and a more volatile vote (Lilleker, 2005). Thus the mechanics of branding are important, as perceptions cannot be changed overnight.

FURTHER READING

For an introduction to branding see J. Kapferer (1997) *Strategic Brand Management*, London: Kogan Page. On party branding see A. Lock and P. Harris (1996) 'Political marketing – vive la difference', *European Journal of Marketing*, 30 (10/11): 14–24. A critique of rebranding is offered by D.G. Lilleker (2005) 'The impact of political marketing on internal party democracy', in D. McHugh and C. Needham, *Parliamentary Affairs Special Edition: The Future of the Party System*. Oxford: Oxford University Press.

political communication

45

Broadcasting/ Narrowcasting

> *Broadcasting, a common feature of the communication of political actors in both pluralist, media-centred democracies as well as authoritarian regimes, is any communication which is directed towards the masses. Therefore different communication modes as diverse as political advertising, campaign leaflets, speeches to the parliament, press releases or any political statement that can be reported by the media can come under the heading of broadcasting. This means that all such communication must be designed to appeal to all segments of the electorate and cannot exclude or offend any one group.*

ORIGINS AND LINKS

Broadcasting is normally associated solely with the media industry, and in particular radio and television companies' communication to their audiences. However, we should not forget that those that create the news, in particular, organisations that use **news management** techniques to gain favourable coverage and the transmission of their **messages**, are also in the business of broadcasting. In a **media-centred democracy**, in which all political communication is **mediated** prior to reaching the public, all political communication is automatically viewed as being broadcasting. Clearly not all communication is broadcast, the media choose what is news and what aspects to broadcast; however, the fact that everything that is said or done in the public arena can be broadcast means that great efforts are made to ensure that everything that can be broadcast is packaged in the way intended by the originator.

The history of political communication is necessarily a history of the mass media. While avoiding reducing the **professionalisation** debate to **technological determinism**, we can see that as the mass media has evolved, increasing its reach, so politicians have had to be increasingly aware of media **audiences** and the way in which the media operates. Thus politicians have had to adapt to newspapers, radio, television, and now the Internet as the media through which to reach the public. Equally in some countries, such as the USA, politicians are able to exploit paid-for channels of mass communication, so communicating directly to the public, though political advertisements can still be mediated through news coverage. In contrast, politicians in the newer democracies in parts of eastern Europe, South America and Asia are adapting to **pluralism** and the freedom of the media. Thus the concerns of broadcasting are central to the work of a modern political communicator.

KEY FEATURES

Academically the practice of broadcasting is an accepted part of the political sphere. Broadcasting is a central aspect to the public service function of governments, often via a public service broadcasting corporation such as the BBC or the French TV station RTF. It is also recognised that in a pluralist democracy all parties who compete for elections should have access to broadcasting. However, democratic politicians, often faced with an independent and investigative media, are reconsidering the utility of speaking to the mass public in a single voice. Budgetary constraints ensure that the majority of political communication is broadcast via the media; there are, however, attempts to introduce an alternative form of reaching the public: narrowcasting.

Narrowcasting involves direct communication towards key groups, or segments, within the electorate. At a simplistic level politicians can target key groups through magazines or newspapers with a distinct readership. For example, UK Prime Minister Tony Blair wrote articles in the *Sun* newspaper in order to communicate with the affluent working-class Conservative voter. In a similar attempt, but on this occasion to target female voters, Russian President Vladimir Putin inserted broadcasts between soap operas and reality television shows. More sophisticated methods for narrowcasting involve the use of email, e-newsletters, SMS text messages or direct mail, where individuals can be targeted with tailored party political messages. This has evolved from the practice of tailoring election communication to the state or constituency level. However, postmodernity has introduced an extra and more personalised and individualistic variant of communication, whereby the individual is seen as the prime unit of politics and needs to be communicated to via the most appropriate media and using individually tailored and relevant language and messages.

THE ACADEMIC AND PRACTICAL DEBATES

Politicians will argue that the more that they are able to deliver non-mediated communication the better, because the media distort political messages and encourage public cynicism. However, beyond a few countries where paid advertising is allowed and affordable by the parties, it is difficult to conduct much non-mediated communication. Though, of course, the increased public access to the Internet, currently 59 per cent for Europe, and its raised importance as a source of political information during the 2004 US presidential election, means that new routes are offering more potential. Such developments will necessitate a greater focus on strategic narrowcasting towards key voter segments in key areas.

The problem with narrowcasting is that it is not a secure channel of communication. The media still receive the material, even if it is second hand, and can report on it. The Canadian Liberal Party received much negative publicity for mailing pledge cards on gun laws to different voters that contained opposing promises. Therefore care has to be taken. However, the cost of narrowcasting is prohibitive and thus broadcasting appears to have a secure future until the Internet, the only medium that offers free access to the masses, reaches critical mass as a communication tool.

FURTHER READING

Experiments by Gerber and Green in the USA offer some indications as to the efficacy of narrowcast communication; see A.S. Gerber and D.P. Green (2000) 'The effects of canvassing, direct mail and telephone contact on voter turnout', *American Political Science Review*, 94 (3): 653–63. See also B.J. Doherty and M.C. Anderson (2004) 'Message tailoring in Spanish: Courting Latino voters in the 2000 presidential advertising campaign', in D.A. Shultz (ed.), *Lights, Camera, Campaign!: Media, Politics and Political Advertising*. New York: Peter Lang.

key concepts

48

Campaigns/ Campaigning

> *A campaign is a series of events all designed to communicate to an audience and garner support from that audience. Campaigns are used by a wide range of actors, both commercial and political, and are designed to win over the audience through a range of increasingly sophisticated techniques.*

ORIGINS AND LINKS

Campaigning originated with competition between groups in society for the support of the public. During the 16th and 17th centuries Europe saw churches competing, each using campaigning techniques, during wars nations compete both militarily and through **propaganda**, and during elections political candidates, parties and pressure groups compete over issues for public support. Campaigns can be distinguished based on the number of actors involved and the number of issues (see Figure 5).

Referenda and elections are normally fought by actors opposing one another ideologically; however, they may not be the only competitors. For example, referenda that have taken place across the European Union on membership of the monetary union have also seen the Union itself running information campaigns. Similarly, pressure groups can

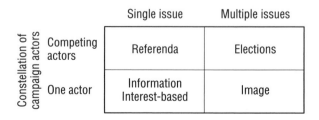

		Single issue	Multiple issues
Constellation of campaign actors	Competing actors	Referenda	Elections
	One actor	Information Interest-based	Image

Figure 5   *A typology of political campaigns (adapted from Farrell and Schmit-Beck, 2004: 4)*

political communication

49

disseminate communication that impacts on other's campaigns. However, in politics we tend to focus on national elections, as these are seen as the most important type of campaign within the field of political communication because of the high levels of competition, spending and sophistication. The reason for the sophistication is the complexity of an election contest, as is illustrated by the model in Figure 6.

The model shows that the strategy originates with political actors, the leadership of the party or the candidate and their advisors, but is shaped by the media and organisational context of the campaign (hostility from the tabloids or the members for example) and then also by voter opinion. The modern campaign is, therefore, a highly marketised event, where media reaction, organisational responses and voter opinion are all factored into the design as part of an ongoing process.

The issue for politicians, as noted by Farrell and Schmitt-Beck

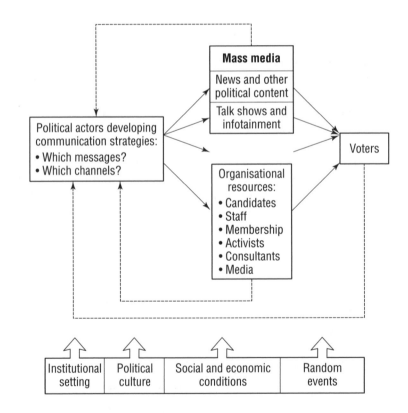

Figure 6 *A model of campaigning (adapted from Farrell and Schmit-Beck, 2002: 6)*

(2002: 9), is the level of control over messages which has to be factored into campaign design alongside the unexpected events that also impact on voter opinion. While there should be total control over messages that come out of the organisation (on the doorsteps or their websites for example) and through advertisements, news values impact on the way that campaigns are reported by the media. Equally candidates are less able to set the agenda when they participate in interviews for news programmes or for popular culture programming.

KEY FEATURES

The key features of what is described as the campaign in the postmodern era are dealt with in greater detail under the discussion of Americanisation and professionalisation. However, the key points, with appropriate illustrative examples are as follows:

- *Campaigns are centrally orchestrated but fought locally.* The close 2004 presidential election contest saw both candidates spend around $22 million just in the state of Ohio courting the floating voters and getting their own supporters to the polling booths.
- *The increased use of professional campaign units and consultants.* The UK Conservatives set up a war room, created a telephone canvassing unit worthy of any cold-calling sales operation and employed the services of Australian consultant Lynton Crosby, who was instrumental in the success of Australian Prime Minister John Howard in 2001, in their 2005 election campaign.
- *The use of market intelligence.* To design, test and redesign the campaign, including testing effectiveness and reaction. The French president, Jacques Chirac, used Ipsos in 2002; less well-funded parties rely on freely available information published by outside pollsters.
- *Media management.* To ensure the messages are transmitted to the audience; hence spin-doctor has become a global term, even within states with large numbers of parties such as Denmark.
- *Narrowcasting.* In an attempt to reach the individual, and not just the mass audience, parties tailor messages in the same way as producers of consumer goods; this was particularly effective for the Canadian regional party *Bloc Quebecois*.
- *The permanent campaign.* When in government, or as an opposition party, it is necessary to have a constant presence and promote the image of the party if not its policy issues.

While many examples, and further aspects, could be highlighted, these six features encapsulate the modern campaign. It is also worth adding, however, the importance of having an early start. The American model sees a year-long campaign starting with primaries which select the presidential candidate, then leading into the race for the presidency itself. This necessitates a high-spending, highly media-focused campaign. This is also spreading. The French primary and run-off stages also promote a long campaign; while in the UK, Prime Minister Blair set the campaign in motion on 20 December 2004, despite the election date only being rumoured to be 5 May 2005. Such unprecedented moves in non-US style systems, suggest that longer campaigns are becoming a feature.

THE ACADEMIC AND PRACTICAL DEBATES

While there are various debates that centre on the extent to which the professionalised model is better, using various measures, there is a more fundamental question about campaigning: does it work? While we know that post-dealignment few are rigidly expected to support one party on ideological grounds, the vote may still be decided during the permanent campaign. One party or candidate may have earned more trust, appear more credible and seem more like a leader of government than the competitors, as George W. Bush was able to in the US in 2004; hence the intense period of campaigning may well be a waste of money, time and resources.

Some evidence suggests that the voter builds up political attitudes from everyday experiences of political outputs; thus we judge the government on our experiences of local health provision, levels of crime or quality of life issues (Popkin, 1991). Further works highlight the importance of our everyday conversations and socialisation between family members (Lenart, 1994), or even complete strangers (Graber, 2001). This evidence is underpinned by the recognition that every member of the media audience face information overload, thus they look to a source they trust for cues on how to vote. Equally, with the postmodern electorate and the media being fragmented, campaign effects are reduced anyway, and so these non-mediated and apolitical influences become more important to us as they are all that are actually received.

Persuasive, contrasting evidence can be found in a range of studies of campaign effects. While long-term effects of permanent campaigning: aiming to establish an image of trust, gaining message recall and building support are not forgotten, there are voter segments that are influenced by the actual election campaign period, some of whom wait until then to make their voting decision. These are the late deciders, those who seek their cues from the campaign and seek emotional or economic stimuli which will help them make a decision. However, the broader electorate also are effected by campaign communication: it is therefore useful to look at the aims of campaigns and how these can effect the audience.

The first role of a campaign is to raise the salience of an issue, usually one that is central to a party's programme. This can set the agenda on an issue owned by the party or set up a counter argument from opponents, these are referred to as wedge issues, which help separate competitors from one another in voters' minds. Either way the electorate is primed to think of an issue, contextualised by the party's messages on it, and so in the future should link the party, the message and the issue, particularly if they care about the issue and identify with the message. The capture of the law and order issue by the UK's Labour Party was a direct result of its ability to seize the agenda due partly to Tony Blair's fairly authoritarian record as the party's home affairs spokesperson.

Secondly, there is a persuasive role. For example, during the referendum on Denmark joining the European Monetary Union the campaign run by right- and left-wing fringe parties, including the nationalist Danish People's Party, the Socialist People's Party, and the Christian People's Party was successful in convincing the Danish people that monetary union would be bad for the economy and the state, and especially for the particularism of Denmark's welfare system.

Thirdly, campaigns can promote recognition for a candidate; a role performed for presidential challengers in the US. They are able to provide the candidate with an image, allow the opportunity to set out policies and enable the voters to decide which candidate is likely to be the best at the job.

Finally, campaigns act as a reminder for supporters. Although it is argued that partisanship and political awareness act as mediating factors on campaign effects, people still need motivating to vote. For this reason parties engage in much local campaigning aimed at getting out their vote as well as converting floating voters into supporters, and attacking their opponents. Local activism is deemed important as it makes a campaign relevant, gives the voters a feeling of importance and permits interpersonal communication between voters and the candidate or party. It is also argued that the lack of such activity depresses turnout and deactivates voter segments.

It is argued, however, that campaigns are stressing the wrong elements.

While we talk of Americanisation, the one key factor in a US presidential campaign is the live candidate debate. This allows candidates to debate issues and be compared on an equal platform by the audience. Simon (2002) argues that this is important to voters. However, most other nation's polities block such events in the name of preventing the dumbing down of political discourse and the reduction of debate to simple oppositionalism. Others argue that leaders who refuse such a challenge are scared of losing: thus even this becomes a party political issue during an election campaign.

Looking at the studies of election campaigning we can see there is clear evidence that they have some effect. As with many other forms of communication, it seems we know that some of the campaigning activities work, but we are not sure which activities these are. However, while it is often argued that campaigning has some effect, campaigns are also criticised in the grounds that they often talk past one another and past the voters, not really permitting informed choices to be made at the ballot box. Few solutions are offered to this conundrum.

FURTHER READING

A good comparative analysis of elections is provided by David M. Farrell and Rudiger Schmitt-Beck (2002) *Do Political Campaigns Matter? Campaign Effects in Elections and Referendum*. London: Routledge). Voter behaviour is explored further in D. Graber (2001) *Processing Politics: Learning from Television in the Internet Age*. Chicago: University of Chicago Press; S. Lenart (1994) *Shaping Political Attitudes: The Impact of Interpersonal Communication and Mass Media*. London: Sage; S. Popkin (1991) *The Reasoning Voter*. Chicago: University of Chicago Press; Adam F. Simon (2002) *The Winning Message: Candidate Behaviour, Campaign Discourse and Democracy. Cambridge*: Cambridge University Press.

key concepts

Civil/Civic Society

Though different concepts, these are interrelated within the study of political communication and so it is worth considering features of both simultaneously. Civil society relates to the freedom individuals enjoy to engage in political activity of their choosing, without institutional or societal constraint; the study of civic society focuses on the rules and norms of a society: how it is ordered. Thus a legitimate system of government will build a civic society founded on freedom, which in turn will encourage the political engagement necessary for a strong civil society.

ORIGINS AND LINKS

These concepts date back to the liberal theories of individuals such as John Locke, Jean Jacques Rousseau and John Stuart Mill. They wrote of a society built upon a social contract, where individual freedoms were guaranteed in exchange for security of property and person. While the nature of freedoms is naturally flexible, depending on the laws of a society, and the definition of security may have been broadened to encompass state provision of health care and welfare benefits, this basis prevails in the western liberal democratic model. There are more contemporary debates regarding the role of the state in the maintenance of a civil society: conservatives would argue economic freedom to be the basis for political freedom (Schecter, 2000); in contrast Marxists see the state as the enabler of individuals to act as 'good civic citizens' (Etzioni, 1995). Postmodernism, supported by Third Way theorists such as Anthony Giddens (1998), argues from a more centrist position. Economic freedoms sit alongside state intervention, both of which enable individuals, to the extent of their ability, to participate in politics, while the combination of freedoms and support will ensure legitimisation of the system.

It is debated to what extent society is truly free, to what extent civic society can be manufactured and what restrictions on individual freedoms can be imposed without breaking down the false consciousness that

political communication

55

members of society are actually free. While such debates are normally purely speculative and theoretical, the legislation that has been introduced in the US, Spain, Russia and the UK to prevent terrorist acts offers a new practical dimension. Critics of the modern liberal democracy posit that the public thinks they are free, but that political activity is governed and constrained to the extent that no individuals or collectives have any real ability to change or modify the system. Thus civic society, the legitimate controls, when extended, can undermine civil society and lead to public disengagement from political activity.

KEY FEATURES

A fully functioning civil society should feature the following characteristics:

- Political institutions are organic to the society, formed from grassroots activity.
- Political organisations are autonomous from the state and economic interests and are founded on mutual agreement among members.
- Political activity is funded by members contributions or through taxation.
- Political policy is driven by societal need and is based upon group-member values.
- Political organisations have a horizontal decision-making structure, leaders will be 'diviners of the will'.
- Identity of political organisations is clear internally and externally.
- Society is formed on the basis of partnership networks co-operating to improve society.
- Political organisations rely on social capital; members are assets and link them to society.

(adapted from Hodgson, 2004)

Therefore within these characteristics we recognise the mass-party model, founded on member's interests, to be the most effective in building civil society. Communication from such organisations should not be propagandist, internal and external democracy should be encouraged and there should be a continuous and open line of communication between the organisations and institutions, and the public.

THE ACADEMIC AND PRACTICAL DEBATES

In the wake of voter dealignment and the professionalisation of political communication, and related demise of mass-membership parties, the level of civil engagement is questioned. W. Lance Bennet (2000) points to five areas that undermine civil society:

- The role of the media in providing political information, and related desire for infotainment among audiences.
- The rise of 'lifestyle values' above political values, to which is linked the rise of consumerism.
- The decline of collective political experience and action; partly linked to economic voting, also due to the fragmentation of society.
- The global politics of the Internet, so weakening state boundaries and moving political activity outside the nation-state.
- Global citizenship initiatives, aided by the Internet, as well as political organisations that act globally and differ from traditional political organisations due to the lack of representation and accountability.

This does not suggest the death of political engagement, but the shifting away from a civic society based around the nation to a global civil society. This is evidenced by the support for global environmentalist pressure groups, such as Greenpeace, or the anti-capitalism/globalisation movement.

Some nations have made attempts to combat this through civic education. Australia embeds nationhood within the History and Social Studies national curriculum, Taiwan's democracy is nurtured at school through extensive classes in 'civics and morality' while non-secular societies incorporate 'civics' into religious education. Each nation attempts to ensure that systemic legitimacy is an accepted social norm and, as a result, the public choose to participate in the process. However, social theorists argue that such attempts are not far removed from the activities of nations where legitimacy is encouraged through mass propaganda and control over information. The Communist Party of China uses the media to promote itself, to curb public discussions of politics and, so, to maintain the stability of the regime, a tactic employed by many dictatorships that rule on the approval of a largely passive, indoctrinated society.

The fact that such methods can be witnessed in advanced democracies causes many to question the extent to which civic society and civil society are linked in the modern age. It could be argued that they are now in opposition to one another, as civil society moves outside the state, civic society attempts to draw it back, but its only tools for doing so are coercion and indoctrination. In an age of weakened political organisations, many of whom have lost the legitimacy awarded by a mass membership, this is a problem for political parties that claim to be democratic yet appear to be elitist managers who are disconnected from those they claim to represent and whose existence is solely for the purpose of gaining and retaining power. Thus what we must ask is do we recognise our political leaders in this negative perception of the modern liberal democracy?

FURTHER READING

On the debates of the role of the state see A. Etzioni (1995) *The Spirit of Community*. London: Fontana; D. Schecter (2000) *Sovereign States or Political Communities?* Manchester: Manchester University Press; A. Giddens (1998) *The Third Way: The Renewal of Social Democracy*. Cambridge: Polity. For discussions of the extent to which civil society can be manufactured see L. Hodgson (2004) 'Manufactured civil society: counting the cost', *Critical Social Policy*, 24 (2): 139–64; M. Keane (2001) 'Broadcasting policy, creative compliance and the myth of civil society in China', *Media, Culture and Society*, 23: 783–98. The role of communication, and in particular new media, is introduced in W. Lance Bennett (2000) 'Introduction: Communication and civic engagement in comparative perspective', *Political Communication*, 17: 307–12. This introduces a special volume that includes many studies that would be of use in exploring these themes further.

Consumerism/ Consumerisation

Political consumerism primarily describes the way in which the public see political outputs, or the outcome of policy, as consumers: thus they judge politics in a similar way to many other, commercial service providers. It can also be attached to the phenomenon of the public employing direct political action against government, or the corporate sphere, through their consumer buying behaviour.

ORIGINS AND LINKS

The consumerisation of political behaviour is one way of explaining the current attitudes of the public to politics post-**dealignment**. It is the result of a number of interrelated factors converging: the electoral professionalism and managerialism of political parties; the perceived distance between politics and the public with the end of the mass party; and the rise of the consumer as sovereign as a result of the market orientation adopted firstly by corporate and latterly political organisations. The power of the consumer, in a highly competitive market-place, is well documented (Gabriel and Lang, 2000). As many commentators have noted, some aspects of consumer buying behaviour have an explicitly political dimension: for example, the refusal to buy real fur; demanding ethical business practice; the desire for corporate social responsibility. These areas find consumers buying products which match their political ideas, so sending powerful messages to producers that flout public demands to change their practice (Micheletti et al., 2003).

A somewhat more recent development has been the consumerisation of political activity and voting behaviour. This is highlighted in Lees-Marshment (2004), where she notes that the UK public expect high levels of service in welfare policy such as education, health-care provision and the maintenance of law and order. This introduces the concept of **political marketing** to political party behaviour, as a **permanent campaign** is waged to ensure customer satisfaction in welfare provision, and so satisfaction in government policy. Such consumerism is a common feature in neo-liberal western society (Marcuse, 1964). Its increasing pervasion has changed the nature of political policy making, the related communication, the behaviour of the tiers of government, as well as the way in which they are treated by the media.

The problem for the political sphere is that within a postmodern society, where symbols and imagery are argued to have greater power than fact and truth, due to the shifting nature of fact and truth, individuals use shortcuts provided by a range of media to build their personal ideological framework. As was the case with the election of Blair in the UK, Haider in Austria and to some extent President Vladimir Putin in Russia expectations, founded on constructed perceptions of the future, were far higher than reality would allow. Appeals by politicians to aesthetics and symbols are able to position them within the ideological framework held by individuals. However, this then places them on a par with consumer goods; hence they are judged in the same way. While Putin has been able, through slick political skills and media controls, to retain his image in Russia, Haider fell quickly and Blair's image was soon tarnished. Thus political consumerism increases the instability and volatility of the electoral contest and increases the use of marketing techniques within the political sphere.

KEY FEATURES

It is important to recognise that there are three distinct groups important in the area of political communication, each of which promote consumerism in their own ways. These are the political organisations, the electorate and the media. Each will be discussed briefly to explain the impact of consumerism.

Political organisations see themselves as the victims of consumerism, it is something they have to react to. This leads to change, yet often change takes them in a direction that is not satisfactory either to members and supporters or to those who need to be persuaded. However, the rise of the political consumer underpins much of the **professionalisation** of party organisation and political communication and the rise of political marketing. Politicians, however, find themselves ill-equipped to deal with the social changes they face, so they hire consultants. These will come from fields that have become accustomed to the social changes, and their remit will be to adapt political activity to the new social landscape. As a result parties will be more interested in public opinion, as were corporations before them; they will develop policies and messages relevant to the key segments they aim to win over; communication will aim to control expectations; and delivery on promises will be a priority. Two quotes illustrate this. The first is from an interview with an Australian management consultant working with a political party portfolio: '[the party] must understand what the consumer wants from them, not promise the earth, but ensure that they are able to offer benchmarks against which the public can measure their performance. This is the basis of any transaction, which politics is now seen as being' (personal communication). The second is from an advisor working with an international environmental pressure group: 'We ask for donations, those who donate expect a return on the things they believe in. If we fail to be proactive we cannot ask again. Though we do not sell a product, our services are being bought.' (personal communication) Thus political organisations are forced to face consumerism head on and adapt their behaviour to suit.

The public are, therefore, more demanding. They have expectations and demand that they are met. They will withhold their support from a party or organisation either by not being active or by not voting for them. They expect that their demands are met, and judge this against individual benchmarks, hence organisations' attempts to control these expectations. Political organisations, however, find it difficult to control consumerist perceptions, often due to the role of the media.

The media has become increasingly market-oriented, each organisation attempts to provide its core audience with 'what they want, when they want it, in the way they want'. Studies have shown that normal, everyday, politicking has been sidelined. Political organisations usually only gain coverage when they fit with existing agendas, act in a way that conforms to set news values or, which is more often the case, when they can provide entertaining coverage. Dutch populist Pim Fortuyn was able to garner controversial media coverage, while remaining loved by the people; though he was never able to gain a majority in the parliament. In contrast, successive stories of sexual impropriety or taking cash for supporting causes tarnished the image of John Major's 1992–97 UK Conservative government and of Gerhard Schroeder's in Germany. Similarly, media investigations also led to the resignation in the UK of Labour ministers Stephen Byers, Peter Mandelson and David Blunkett. This dumbing down of politics is argued to be what the public want from the tabloids; however, television's market orientation is seen as also promoting infotainment at the expense of real political news. Hence consumers are not given all the information required to make a sensible consumer decision and are often presented with negative representations of all electoral competitors; thus they end up rejecting electoral activity in favour of more consumer-focused political power.

THE ACADEMIC AND PRACTICAL DEBATES

While the effects of political consumerisation may be felt sharply by political organisations, many agree they have benefited as have minority ideas in society. The rise of post-materialist values – environmentalism, social equality, human rights and personal integrity – mean that the political agenda has been changed, arguably by consumers themselves (Micheletti et al., 2003). There is a raft of traditional ideas and policies that the new, socially conscious civil society will not accept, thus political organisations are formed to defend these new values and electoral parties must alter the focus of their policy. This is particularly the case with ethical dimensions included in a number of foreign policy statements following the G5 summit in 1998. At this meeting the most powerful nations on the planet decided they would focus on solving global problems, particularly Third World debt, poverty and social exclusion as well as more traditional concerns such as international crime and terrorism.

The problem at the heart of this argument is the extent of real commitment among governments to post-materialist values, particularly in the light of 9/11 and the war on terrorism. Political parties are argued to use their slick communication techniques, designed by advertising and public relations experts, to pay lip service to the environment or Third World debt, while doing nothing substantial once elected. If writers such as Gabriel and Lang, and before them social theorists such as Marcuse and Baudrillard, are correct in arguing that consumerism is both empowering and distracting, then governments may have to act with more commitment, work to consumers' benchmarks, and be accountable. However, this contrasts with the dominant theories of voter behaviour. Economic models suggest we make decisions based on individualistic concerns and not post-materialist values, therefore perhaps parties and governments can get away with focusing on the economy, or the dollar in the pocket, and the consumer will be happily distracted from taking a more activist role as a political consumer. Perhaps this nicely evidences the complexity of the modern political consumer, sometimes they want value driven politics, at other times personal benefits; if an accurate reflection of current society this represents a significantly different, and more complex, political terrain than that which most textbooks lead us to understand.

FURTHER READING

On the political consumer see Micheletti, Stolle and Follesdal (eds) (2003) *Politics, Products and Markets: Exploring Political Consumerism Past and Present*. New York: Transaction Books. On consumer power see Gabriel and Lang (2000) *The Unmanageable Consumer*. London: Sage. On political consumerism, and the effect on the tiers of UK government see Jennifer Lees-Marshment (2004) *The Political Marketing Revolution*. Manchester: Manchester University Press. On political consumerism and neo-liberal western society see Henri Marcuse (1964) *The One Dimensional Man*. London: Routledge.

Cynicism

Cynicism relates to disbelief, mistrust and scepticism. When pertaining to political communication we think of it as a culture, where the audience receiving political messages are more likely to view them with disbelief than with belief, in other words, the public is sceptical of everything politicians say.

ORIGINS AND LINKS

The study of public cynicism has arisen alongside studies of dealignment and the increased media criticism of politics. Normatively, we hear that the public view political communication as another part of the diet of sales-related communication, of which they are sceptical anyway. Media criticism of politics and politicians, stories framed in discourses of sleaze, **spin** and scandal, exacerbate the atmosphere of mistrust, and so politics is seen to lack efficacy and politicians are largely given a low rating on issues of public trust.

While some commentators perceive cynicism to be the result of the increased **professionalisation** of political communication, others see it as a causal factor; therefore debates often centre on which came first or did the two evolve side by side. Others relate it to the changing **news values**,

political communication

63

the breakdown in political **source–reporter relations** and a consequence of **news management** and **spin** strategies. Combating cynicism is now a key role of political communication, hence we hear of politicians projecting greater **authenticity** and adopting **political marketing** concepts in an attempt to reconnect to their audience.

KEY FEATURES

Measuring the level of cynicism within the public sphere is difficult and often locked into contextual factors. For example, trust in politicians in the UK during the events surrounding the Hutton Inquiry, or in France during the trial of the former prime minister, Juppe, will have been lower than at normal times. However, such instances may also have a lasting negative effect on perceptions of efficacy and will lead to behavioural changes among the electorate. Some argue low turnout is one such indicator, others claim this to be a sign of satisfaction in the democratic process and there being little desire for change; thus little is clear in terms of how the voters are affected.

It may be that the shift from national, electoral politics to local and issue-based politics reflects a cynicism in the former that has changed the nature of civil society. Thus those who would pursue political activism will reject the deceitful electoral political organisations in favour of those that they trust, and that support causes they care about. This argument is somewhat tautological, however; if the public have rejected the current parties should they not be focusing on alternatives. Is this why parties such as Le Pen's Front Nationale was promoted to the run-off in the 2002 French presidential election? This is difficult to assess, although some commentators suggest there is an anti-politics political movement, one that is rejecting party politics; some link this to cynicism, others find that link problematic.

THE ACADEMIC AND PRACTICAL DEBATES

Pippa Norris's work highlights that the public do not always become disenchanted by political scandal, spin or negativity. Contrary to the accepted wisdom, she argues that the increased focus on infotainment leads to greater interest in politics. While this may include non-electoral activism, it does not lead the public to turn away from electoral politics; but they are more selective about their participation. Therefore it is changes in society, and the extent of civic duty, that dictates turnout; cynicism is the wrong focus of study.

What we do know is that the public can become cynical of political communication, sometimes due to media coverage. However, there are a number of caveats here. First, and importantly, cynicism can be context specific, for example during the Danish referendum on joining the European Single Currency (De Vrees and Semetko, 2004). Furthermore, the propensity for developing cynical attitudes towards individual politicians or organisations may be mediated by personal feelings, previous communication or other factors belonging to the individual. Finally, cynicism is not about all political communication, and could be linked to debates on whether we reject that which is irrelevant to our lives. Therefore we can conclude that although cynicism appears to be increasing, and perhaps spiralling out of control, we remain unsure as to the cause, but an assumption is that it is related to the public intake of mediated information.

Relating this to theories of media effects, the fact that the mass media focus on political scandal, and themselves argue that this creates cynicism, we could posit that it is a self-fulfilling prophecy: that the media both create cynicism and then feed it. However, it could also be a media myth, that actually only the politicians that are implicated in scandals earn cynical attitudes, the rest we treat with the same level of trust or disdain that we would have awarded them anyway. Before we can make an empirical judgement we must first identify the level of cynicism that exists, then identify the cause and then test it over time to assess whether it is deepening or context-specific. Until that time, we must treat the notion of a cynical society itself with a healthy level of cynicism.

FURTHER READING

The key text here is J.N. Capella and K.H. Jamieson (1997) *Spiral of Cynicism: The Press and the Public Good*. New York: Oxford University Press. The cynical public is mentioned in many other texts, for examples see C.H. De Vreese and H.A. Semetko (2004) 'Cynical and engaged: Strategic campaign coverage, public opinion and mobilization in a referendum', *Communication Research*, 29 (6): 615–41. For a refutation of the media effects thesis see P. Norris (2000) *A Virtuous Circle*. Cambridge, Cambridge University Press.

Dealignment

Dealignment describes the process by which partisanship, or loyalty to one party, among the electorate has reduced over the last half-century. It was once the case that voters held strong, often lifelong, attachments to one political party, often due to its perceived link to a social class. As class divisions are eroded, parties have arguably converged around a managerialist model which reduces ideological differences between parties, thus voter loyalty is far more flexible and can shift between elections, and there is a much reduced base of supporters that parties can rely on to support them at elections.

ORIGINS AND LINKS

Dealignment entered academic parlance following studies into partisan attachments during the 1960s. What was noted then, and subsequently, was that fewer individuals claimed to be unquestioningly supportive of one party, and fewer still believed attachments to be lifelong. This means that campaign communication can be far more effective and so must be more strategic; aimed to win over support rather than remind voters to vote. The period when dealignment began is open to some interpretation, and can be nation-specific: it begins in the 1940s in New Zealand, in the US its roots are in the 1950s, while across Europe it is the 1970s, and yet some nations did not experience quantifiable shifts until the 1980s. However, dealignment, and the rise of the floating voter, is now a global phenomenon.

The concept is central to our understanding of **campaigning**, and underpins discussions of **professionalisation** and the rise of **electoral professionalism** and **political marketing**. It has also had a profound impact upon **cultural capital** and **civic society**, though not a necessarily negative one but more one not defined along party political lines.

THE KEY FEATURES

With dealignment has come the floating voter, a voter with no party political allegiance who is inclined to view politics as part of the daily diet of consumerism. The individualistic view has provided evidence for economic and rationale choice theories of voting, which tell us that we vote not for a party due to ideological attachments but on the basis of a judgement of which party will be best for 'me' the voter and 'my' personal circumstances. This does not reduce attachment to social policy, as voters still see themselves as a part of society; what they seek is the best social policy for them on their terms. While new classes have formed, such as the new working class based in the service industry rather than manufacturing, their political attachments may evidence group identities; however, these are more related to gender, race or perceived economic status than social class (Lilleker, 2002). Hence those who feel unprivileged may still vote for a left-wing party because they feel they will be better off economically, but the allegiance is weak and dependent on perceptions of confidence, trust and responsibility.

The loss of a core group of loyal voters has led parties to be more concerned with communication, both to sell them as 'the best party' for a particular social group and to discover what it is that will make a particular social group vote for them. Parties increasingly attempt to identify floating voters, segment them and narrowcast towards groups of them. Thus the professionalisation of political communication and consequent use of marketing research and communication flows from voter dealignment.

THE ACADEMIC AND PRACTICAL DEBATES

The attachment between social classes and political parties could be described as a romantic view at any period in post-1945 history, and even before in many stable democratic nations. European Communist parties attracted both the least and the best educated, as did many other socialist parties. Right-wing parties, on the other hand, attracted middle-class entrepreneurs as well as conservative members of the working class seeking to 'better their lot' in life. The 1960s brought indications that there was a breakdown in allegiances. The influential Affluent Worker studies, conducted by a team led by Professor Goldthorpe in the mid-1960s, which studied workers in UK car manufacturing plants, showed the beginning of a steady decline, yet many argue that this was not serious until the 1990s and certainly did not effect party behaviour. Across Europe, however, it is now a given that voters are far more disloyal than at any period previously and, as a partial result, are far more disengaged from electoral politics (Mair et al., 2004).

Further questions relate to the fact that some voters appear to be realigning rather than rejecting all notions of partisanship. The increased choice in many countries operating with proportional representation voting systems encourages these shifts, and allows voters to be more consumerist as well as tactical when deciding how to cast their vote. However, the level of non-partisanship remains high and appears to be increasing; a trend some link to reductions in turnout and apparent rejection of electoral politics in favour of more individualistic causes.

Whether the latter is a factor caused by dealignment, or an underlying social cause for party loyalty to witness an ongoing decrease, is an interesting conundrum. Thus, while academics accept dealignment as fact, and recognise loyalty as shifting and unstable, its effects and the successes of responses are open to some discussion.

FURTHER READING

A discussion of the impact of dealignment on parties across Europe can be found in P. Mair, W.G. Muller and F. Plasser (2004) *Political Parties and Electoral Change*. London, Sage. For a study of the impact on voting behaviour among the 'new' working class in the UK see D.G. Lilleker (2002) 'Whose Left? Working-class political allegiances in post-industrial Britain', *International Review of Social History*, Suppl. 10: 65–86; for a study with a broader focus see R. Dalton, S. Flanigan and P. A. Beck (1984) *Electoral Change in Advanced Industrial Societies: Realignment or Dealignment?* Princeton, NJ: Princeton University Press. The effects on political communication are discussed in many texts on professionalisation and political marketing, see for example B.I. Newman and R.M. Perloff (2004) 'Political marketing: Theory, research, and applications', in L.L. Kaid (ed.), *Handbook of Political Communication Research*. London: Lawrence Erlbaum.

key concepts

Dumbing Down

Dumbing down is a term used to describe not only the way in which, primarily, the media report political news, making the presentation of politics similar to that of popular culture, but also to the way in which political communication has responded. Academics find political communicators designing their communication for media consumption, promoting presentation, style and personalisation over policy and serious debate.

ORIGINS AND LINKS

Dumbing down was one of the buzzwords of the 1990s (Barnett, 1998) and was first deployed to critique a whole range of key societal structures. Education was the first target, as gaining qualifications, such as A levels, appeared to be getting easier, the term then began to move through media reports until it become a catch-all definition. In terms of the media, such criticisms were defined as the tabloidisation of news, what Franklin (1997) called 'newszak'. This referred to the increasing focus on low culture, celebrity, sports personalities and sex scandal, and the move away from serious political coverage. In the UK the disappearance of parliamentary coverage was bemoaned, and, it has been argued, the news reduced to covering the ephemera of society, as for example the global television phenomenon that is *Big Brother*, and the attendant focus on the winners and losers in the media. While such criticisms have always been levelled at a certain class of newspaper, the tabloids – the US *Daily News*, the UK's *Sun* or the French daily *Le Figaro* for example – television news has received similar approbation. Living up to descriptions such as an opiate, 'bubble gum for the eyes', television is now accused of shifting **news values**, as well as **frames** and **agendas**, to focus on **popular culture**, and leaving the audience depoliticised. However, more recently, and as the political communications consultants attempt to get their clients into the headlines, similar criticisms are levelled at political actors and organisations as well.

As it is argued that our reliance on television for information reduces our intellectual capacity, it is equally suggested that the reliance of political organisation on television to reach a mass audience leads political communication to adopt televisual norms and culture. As a result, politicians are complicit in the transformation of politics from a serious business to a soap opera. Personality and **style**, emotions and **aesthetics**, become prioritised; equally political policy is shaped by the 24-hour news cycle and timed to receive maximum favourable media coverage.

KEY FEATURES

It is often argued that dumbing down is happening to us all imperceptibly, and that it is only when we compare news coverage and political communication now, in 2005, with that of 10 or 20 years ago, that we are able to detect differences. The media within that time has devoted far less time or space to 'high' politics, the making and discussing of policy in the committee rooms or parliaments. In place of this, it is argued, we find celebrity gossip or editorials on the process of politics. What we are missing is access to the debates that underpin policy making, thus the public sphere becomes more infotainment-oriented and disengages from politics (Dahlgren, 1995).

Political communication, in turn, attempts to fit to the media logic. The necessity of publicity leads to policy being reduced to the soundbite; thus the slogan 'putting people first', originally popularised by US presidential candidate Bill Clinton in 1994, was also adopted by the leader of the Brazilian PT party Lula da Silva. This oversimplification does not end with the soundbite. Policies become personalised around single individuals, either 'ideal' voters or telegenic politicians, and parties are branded using symbolism that lacks substance, while image is prioritised. In the words of one German political consultant: 'Politicians now spend more time learning how to dress, speak and perform on camera than they do about the business of their departments' (personal communication).

THE ACADEMIC AND PRACTICAL DEBATES

Central to Barnett's argument is the question of whether dumbing down is actually reaching out to the everyday public. Barnett argues not, rather that the media fails to provide the public with the objective information required to participate in politics. However, politicians do argue that there is a requirement to talk in a language the public understand and conform to the norms of popular culture in order that they are able to communicate. In other words they need to transmit their image in a mode and at a level that the public want; hence they must 'dumb down' the political debate in order that the public can participate.

There seems to be a vicious cycle in operation here. The media's drive towards a market orientation has led the coverage of politics to emphasise personality, scandal and soap opera-style aspects of political life. This in turn has led political communicators to attempt to adapt their press releases, pseudo-events and promotional activity to the news values and frames. They try to capture the news through the use of dramatic rhetoric, carefully constructed soundbites and stunts; what is not released, as it is not interesting to the media, is the political detail.

The negative results are said to be upon the public. If political news is consumed for the purposes of making informed choices, both about ongoing policy and regarding voting choice, as uses and gratifications theorists suggest, there is a deficit of information. Recent studies of political advertising, the use of soundbites and news management strategies debate the extent and direction of the effect on the public. Some argue that the reduction of political policy to a core message facilitates understanding, that negativity stimulates interest, and that the adversarialism exaggerated in media coverage allows the audience to inspect, dissect and understand policies, manifestoes and their ramifications. The alternative story surrounds the cynicism that exists within society: that politics is irrelevant to everyday life, that single voters cannot have any input, and that politicians are all corrupt and seeking power only. There are no definitive answers to this, only debates, each of which need to be considered in terms of our own understanding and interaction with political communication and its mediation.

FURTHER READING

Background and a critique of the media are provided in S. Barnett (1998) 'Dumbing down or reaching out: Is it tabloidisation wot done it?', in J. Seaton (ed.), *Politics and the Media: Harlots and Prerogatives at the Turn of the Millennium*. London: Blackwell. pp. 75–90; B. Franklin (1997) *Newszak and News Media*. London: Arnold. For a critique of similar trends among political communicators see M. Scammell (1995) *Designer Politics: How Elections Are Won*. London: Macmillan. For a debate on the effect on the public sphere see P. Dahlgren (1995) *Television and the Public Sphere: Citizenship, Democracy and the Media*. London: Sage.

E-representation/ E-politics

E-representation refers to the potential offered by new media for a greater interactivity between the public and political spheres; E-politics refers to the embedding of political activity within the Internet, one that includes public activity as well as established political organisations.

ORIGINS AND LINKS

As every technological advance becomes a mainstream tool, a range of predictions are made. The more conservative will argue that little will change, others will suggest that the world is about to change. So it is with political communication and the World Wide Web. Perhaps those who are less conservative are idealists, with the cynicism, disengagement and general disconnection of the public from politics, some look to e-communications as a possible panacea for the decline in active political interest among the public. Writers in separate fields hypothesise about the effect the Internet could have. Bourdieu, a scholar of literature and art, highlighted that the new media offering electronic communication to the masses, offered 'infinite repertoires of possibility' (1993). In essence, art, literature and high culture could be brought to the masses, as opposed to having to attract the masses to theatres, museums or galleries. Clearly the same can be said of politics. However, it is not about placing web-cams in parliament, it is about the use of the Web for interactive purposes. It is about allowing the public and their political representatives to have what public relations theorists describe as a symmetrical relationship. This essentially means communication is two-way, between public and political, rather than top down and in persuasive form, and both parties are influential and influenced (Jackson and Lilleker, 2004).

Thus at the heart of debates surrounding e-representation or e-politics is a search to find better, more appropriate, forms of **representation** in a modern democracy. Such debates go to the heart of thinking about how politics and its communication should be carried out.

KEY FEATURES

While the traditional media outlets, newspapers and television, offer the opportunity for political communicators to reach a mass audience on a daily basis, the use of mass media is often argued to be unsatisfactory. First, the mass media follow their own agenda, decide what is news and what is not, and will happily frame stories to suit their own editorial purposes; thus there is not a free flow of information from the political sphere into the public domain. However, the second criticism is that the public are no longer satisfied with attempts to create a free flow of information out of politics to the public. They want to interact, have their say and have power; after all, democracy is all about people power. Traditional media cannot facilitate such communications, they are dialogical: from one to the many. However, electronic communication tools allow one-to-one dialogue as well as many-to-many dialogue. It is this feature that advocates of e-representation get excited about.

In practical terms little real many-to-many communication is occurring that can actually be said to be an attempt at enhancing the representativeness of democracy. While political leader's email addresses may be in the public domain, there remains a cynicism as to whether any single emails are read and instigate political change, never mind eliciting a response. Some candidates have used web-logs (blogs) to communicate with voters, while parties have instigated 'listening' programmes, such as the UK's New Labour and the Big Conversation; however, there are questions as to whether this is just a promotional tool or a tool for better representation. Thus the majority of e-politics is conducted by pressure groups and non-electoral groups. The creation of virtual political communities, set up by like-minded individuals with similar sets of concerns, appears to be moving people away from electoral participation as they feel better represented within that online anonymous community.

THE ACADEMIC AND PRACTICAL DEBATES

There are two major critiques of e-representation. The first is a practical one and relates to the uses made of the World Wide Web by the public. Surveys conducted by the Pew Institute in the USA find some positive indications, even though the normative view is that the average Internet user is someone seeking to play interactive games, shop or view pornography. As any form of e-representation requires a critical mass of public engagement, and that this is nowhere near being attained, 'the broadcast media remain far more important [for political parties] in getting one's message across to a large audience' (Gibson et al., 2003: 242). Here we could also raise concerns as to the elitist demographics of those with unrestricted Web access, because unless all citizens have an opportunity to participate then any reliance placed on using electronic communications would actually disenfranchise many voters who are computer illiterate or have few resources. This leads political parties to create websites in order to appear modern, but to use them as little more than an electronic brochure. Few attempts are made at interaction; it is more about having a presence and advertising your wares.

The second critique is more theoretical, and so perhaps more contestable. This is the argument that the virtual nature of e-politics creates a false community. We may feel that we are connected to others, yet we have little real knowledge of other members, or the motives behind the creation of a blog, discussion board, chat room or website. As the Internet facilitates anonymous communication, each of us can create a virtual identity. Just as the Internet facilitates fraud, when someone claims to be something they are not, so it also allows people to appear politically active, committed and caring. Thus we cannot, as Axford (2001) points out, create organisations that are based upon mutual trust and collective identity; we know nothing about those we interact with.

While this makes a lot of sense, relationships are still created using the Internet, and political debate and discussion can be translated into effective direct political action. Just consider the anti-capitalism movement which, through using electronic communications, managed to stage massive demonstrations during meetings of the World Trade Organisation in 2000 and 2001. Jayne Rodgers (2004) also highlights the effective use between anti-nuclear groups coordinating their work and building a mutually supportive community. As with many debates surrounding the applications and effects of the World Wide Web, perhaps it is still too early to tell. At present, however, the 'wired generation', those computer-literate activists, feel they gain representation from participating in e-politics; the vast majority, however, find it business as usual.

On the possibilities see P. Bordieu (1993) *The Field of Cultural Production: Essays on Art and Literature*. Cambridge: Polity. On the potential from a public relations perspective see N. Jackson and D.G. Lilleker (2004) 'Just public relations or an attempt at interaction? British MPs in the press, on the Web and "in your face"', *European Journal of Communication*, 19 (4): 507–33. On party use of the Internet see R. Gibson, P. Nixon and S. Ward (2003) *Political Parties and the Internet: Net Gain?* London: Routledge. The conclusion (pp. 234–43) raises many question covering the potential and viability. E-politics are critiqued in B. Axford (2001) 'The transformation of politics or anti-politics', in B. Axford and R. Huggins, *New Media and Politics*. London: Sage; the power of virtual communities are explored in J. Rodgers (2004) *Spatializing International Politics: Analysing Activism on the Internet*. London: Routledge.

Electoral professionalism

> *Electoral professionalism is the strategy developed by a party whose main aim is electoral success. All elements of the design of the parties' electoral offering are conducted to suit the electoral terrain, particularly voter opinion formation.*

political communication

75

ORIGINS AND LINKS

The term is developed from studies of party behaviour and organisation in the 1950s and 1960s when **dealignment** was seen to be impacting most acutely. Academics noted that as voters became less partisan they sought alternative reasons, for example economic, rational, or even emotional, on which to base their electoral decisions, forcing parties to respond. (Kircheimer, 1956; Inglehart, 1984; Panebianco, 1988; see also Figure 7).

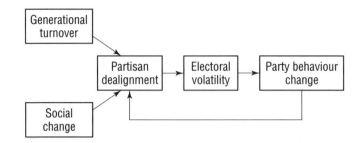

Figure 7   *The process of dealignment (derived from Harrop and Miller, 1987)*

In Figure 7 we see new generations of voters responding to social changes that influence their relationship with political parties and lead to weakening partisanship and increased electoral volatility, the uncertainty that a social group will support one particular party. Parties respond by becoming more professional in their organisation and communication, which in turn has an impact on partisanship, usually by further weakening alignments due to parties focusing on segments of the electorate and not focusing on core or loyal voters due to their reduced number and electoral influence. It is this process that underpins much of the discussion of postmodern political communication.

KEY FEATURES

Panebianco (1988) argued that parties follow a representative bureaucratic model, what can also be defined in terms of managerialism. Leaders act as managers of the party system, as well as of the electorate and the country, if elected. This develops the core functions of the electoral professional party as described by Kircheimer (1956), which are:

- the organisation of the electorate's demands into a programme;
- the selection of electorally attractive representatives;
- the weighing of competing demands to inform collective decisions.

While the root of programmatic messages is the electorate, they are informed by values, though these now also emerge from society. Hence ideology, as understood by the left–right spectrum, is no longer key to identifying parties. Instead they focus on value-laden managerialism, driven by recognition, particularly among European left-wing parties, that they were seen as too extreme by voters on a range of issues. Inglehart's research found that these issues included public ownership of industry, government management of the economy, international aid and control of multinational corporation's powers (Inglehart, 1984). Thus modernisation and professionalisation of parties such as the German Social Democrats, New Labour in the UK, Dutch Labour, and various Communist parties caused a move towards the centre ground.

Communication that flows from these developments follows the postmodern model elucidated within the discussion of Americanisation and professionalisation. However, in terms of its organisation, we find that the electoral professional party will increasingly use consultants from outside the political sphere, from public relations, advertising and marketing, who will manage the communication process. This disempowers party members and activists, making it a more top-down or hegemonic organisational structure controlled by a cadre. It is this characteristic that reduces the democratic nature of the party, leading many to argue that the electoral success is built upon a weak foundation.

THE ACADEMIC AND PRACTICAL DEBATES

While it is argued that the electoral professional party is far more responsive to voter demands, this is critiqued despite the evidence from political marketing literature. Mayhew (1997) argues that professionalisation equates to an erosion of public trust in electoral organisations due to a breakdown in the links between voters, members and the organisational leadership. What Mayhew calls the 'new public', but which could also be called the political consumer, treats the capital-intensive, professionalised communication of political parties as another aspect of its diet of marketing communication. So the audience disengages from the 'self-contained rhetoric of presentation' (Mayhew, 1997, 19).

Parties such as the US Democrats, the Labour Party in the UK, or the New Zealand Labour Party faced long periods of exclusion from office, or in the latter case massive unpopularity following a drift to the right, and so needed to use postmodern techniques of persuasive communication to convince the voters of their ability to govern. Equally, parties who have been within coalitions like the German SPD or the Austrian Socialist Party still found it necessary to shift towards more professionalised modes of communication. However, some of these, in particular the UK Labour Party, have found they have been reduced to a cadre party, lacking a large enough group of activists with the skills to conduct a postmodern campaign. Thus the electoral professional party is a party of parliament only; it lacks a mass-base and as a result lacks a connection to the public sphere.

political communication

Early studies which retain importance are O. Kircheimer (1956) 'The transformation of western European party systems', in M. Weiner and J. LaPalombara (eds), *Political Parties and Political Development*. Princeton: Princeton University Press; A. Panebianco (1988) *Political Parties: Organisation and Power*. London: Cambridge University Press; R. Inglehart (1984) 'The changing structure of political cleavages in western society', in R. Dalton, *Electoral Changes in Advanced Industrial Democracies: Realignment or Dealignment*, Princeton: Princeton University Press). 25–69; M. Harrop and W.L. Miller (1987) *Elections and Voters: A Comparative Introduction*. Basingstoke: Macmillan. Recent studies of elections and parties are all relevant, see, for example, D.M. Farrell and R. Schmidt-Beck (2002) *Do Campaigns Matter?* London: Routledge for a global comparative study; D. Wring (2004) *The Politics of Marketing the Labour Party*. Basingstoke: Palgrave for a case study of New Labour in the UK. Also see Mayhew L. (1997) *The New Public: Professional Communication and the Means of Social Influence*. Cambridge: Cambridge University Press.

Emotionalisation

key concepts

Emotionalisation refers to the introduction of emotion into political communication. Politicians must express emotion and feelings, it is argued, in reaction to public demand for interactions with politics to be an emotional experience.

78

ORIGINS AND LINKS

Traditionally, politics is often perceived as an unemotional, rational, almost cold process of deliberation and decision making. Conversely, sociological studies reveal that members of society often base their decisions on emotional impulses. While choosing a mortgage provider may be based on economic rationality, a whole range of other important decisions are based on less tangible processes of thought. Marriage was once seen as a rational act, whereby a woman could accept the proposal from a man who could offer her security; now even cultures where arranged marriages are the norm are finding such traditions under attack as marriage contracts are founded on love, an illogical and irrational yet highly powerful emotion. Emotional decision making is also related to purchase decisions. It is argued that we have an emotional attachment to a brand, a service provider and also, prior to dealignment, a political party. Thus while decisions on government spending may be based on logic, even if it is the logic of electoral professionalism, society works far more at the emotional level.

The blurring of the boundaries between political communication and **popular culture** injects equally an even greater level of emotion to politics (Richards, 1994). Popular culture, including advertising, plays on and to our emotions; it is the images and **messages** that form our emotional attachments. Thus Richards (2004) argues that political communication should also offer emotional appeals. While this can accentuate style and **aesthetics**, the personalisation of politics, it can also be related to the **dumbing down** of the presentation of political information.

KEY FEATURES

While Richards (1994) can show evidence for an emotional deficit in politics, in the manner of political communication and its decoding by the audience, it is harder to identify what politicians need to do to inject emotion. After all, it is often argued that image and spin have a negative effect on public engagement as well. Richards (2004) points to four elements that would be important for the emotionalisation of political communication, or in his terminology, political discourse:

1   An overt and continuous relevance of politics to real life. This can take place at local or national levels, and is concerned with making political decisions make sense in terms of their effects on the everyday lives of voters.
2   Political communication should show that the politician is a rounded, human being, who shares all the emotions with their audience. Bucy (2000) argues that we judge political leaders on the appropriateness of their display of emotions, deciding on whether they are real or not, and so whether the person is trustworthy.
3   Political communication should tap into emotional currents, so leading debates, including difficult and controversial topics, rather than

avoiding them. This should not be the carefully crafted soundbite, but an ongoing interaction with the hopes, fears and concerns of the masses.

4 Politics should be expressed within an emotional narrative of everyday life, so communication needs to use the language in the same way as the public and policy should be discussed in a way that is sensitive to how the public experience its outcomes.

THE ACADEMIC AND PRACTICAL DEBATES

There is a clear body of evidence which suggests that the audiences of political communication judge what they see and hear according to the way they decode the information. Sociology suggests that emotions come into play far more than our logical or rational persona. Therefore political communication needs to accentuate the humanity of political leaders, their emotions need to be laid bare in order that we identify with them, and they need to express themselves in a way that enforces recognition that they share common emotional experiences with their audience. This does not mean that snapshots of their lives, a baby being born, illness, personal tragedy, should be placed into the public domain, but that there is an ongoing and intrinsic emotional quality to all interactions between voter and political party. However, is there evidence that this works in the world of practical politics?

Certainly parties and individuals that use emotional appeals, often populist parties of the far right, can make electoral gains, though often these are short term. Similarly, politicians with a celebrity status, or who cultivate one, are able to form an attachment with the public that allows them to make mistakes but be forgiven: consider here the revelations that Arnold Schwarzenegger, candidate for Governor of California, groped co-stars, or the Clinton–Lewinsky affair. However, these do not add up to a body of evidence. It is perhaps the reaction to those political actors who lack emotion that is more telling. One often hears of politicians being described as robots because they lack character or are perceived as being cold. Such descriptors suggest a lack of emotion and often, as a consequence, their future in public life is limited. A good example of this is the only French female Prime Minister Edith Cresson. While some journalists suggested she modelled herself on the highly successful UK Prime Minister Margaret Thatcher, her strident tones and abrupt manner were unpopular with the French public and she lasted only six months in the post. The key problem was that the audience did not see her as an authentic woman. Her public persona lacked emotional depth and so those who welcomed the appointment found they did not identify with her. Thus she was rejected by them on the grounds that she was not one of the collective, not a member of the community, because she was not perceived as sharing and expressing the same emotions.

Political science would largely reject the notion of emotional attachments in politics. Many studies find that voting decisions are based on logical and rational economic calculations: we may view a leader favourably but the important question is 'can he or she run the country and its economy well?' Is it possible to draw these positions closer together? The answer is yes. Clearly the rationality of voting behaviour is an accepted phenomenon, choices made in polling booths are never made on the basis of liking an individual, or identifying with them, without knowledge of the policies and the possible effects. But politicians can deliver information in a way that connects with the voters' emotional side. In the wake of the Asian tsunami and attendant tragedy it would seem to be political suicide for any candidate to declare that they cared little for the people affected by the disaster. Similarly many are argued to have concerns that they want potential leaders to respond to. As Bucy notes, by audiences recognising that leaders react to situations in a similar way to them, they are able to make an assessment of whether they will make the right decisions for the nation (2000). Perhaps this encapsulates the complexity of the postmodern voter well, that while they may be seeking the best person to lead a nation, that decision can be based on the way in which we identify with each of the potential candidates. If we relate this to the example of Edith Cresson, French voters felt that her lack of femininity, perhaps maternalism, meant she did not care about the people. Her strident tone and aggressive stance in debates enforced that image, thus she was rejected as the wrong person for the job.

FURTHER READING

On the emotionalisation of popular culture and its links to public decision making see B. Richards (1994) *Disciplines of Delight: The Psychoanalysis of Popular Culture*. London: Free Association Books. On the need for emotionalisation within political communication see E.P. Bucy (2000) 'Emotional and evaluative consequences of inappropriate leader displays', *Communication Research*, 27 (2): 194–226; B. Richards (2004) 'The emotional deficit in political communication', *Political Communication*, (21): 339–52. The importance of personality in politics in a cross-section of political contexts is demonstrated in various chapters in A. King (2002) *Leaders' Personalities and the Outcomes of Democratic Elections*. Oxford: Oxford University Press.

political communication

Framing

Framing describes the practice of thinking about news items and story content within familiar contexts. The media can be instrumental in creating these frames by introducing news items with predefined and narrow contextualisation. Frames can be designed to enhance understanding, or are used as cognitive shortcuts to link stories to the bigger picture.

ORIGINS AND LINKS

The foremost theorist on media framing is Robert Entman, whose study of US news treatment of two plane crashes (1991) and subsequent theoretical work on media framing (1993) directed academic attention towards the contextualisation of news stories as opposed to agenda-setting and the determination of news values. Entman noted that most events are covered globally; however, the way in which events are covered and presented to each audience can lead to a dominant perception emerging. While linear and direct media effects are contested, concerns remain that stories which concentrate purely on the negative consequences, for example, of joining the European Monetary Union in Denmark and the UK result in the public voting against joining without being given access to objective facts.

Audiences may also create their own frames for news items, as well as a wide range of other forms of political communication, marketing communication and popular culture. The idea is that, like the media, they link any event to their knowledge of similar past events; therefore the way they perceive events, interpret their consequences and then organise their thoughts on events are all linked to their consciousness. A simple example could be the global public response to the Asian tsunami of 26 December 2004. While the scale of death, destruction and suffering is unimaginable to most, audience members can think empathically as we have all experienced the loss of a loved one and we can equally feel both the urge to want to help and the personal need for help had we been involved; this can then determine our action. Past events, such as the attacks on the World

Trade Center on 9/11, Third World famine appeals and other crises where loss of life, homelessness, and disease have been tragic corollaries prepare us for the images and can govern our subsequent thoughts and actions.

The media are normally the focus for study as the presentation of information is usually seen as the source of frames, even though they may subsequently be possessed more among the audience than within media reporting. For example, we currently hear that the public disengagement from politics is, if only in part, driven by a process-obsession or game frame. That the media focus on the way in which policy is made rather than the actual policy itself: common stories feature intra-party divisions thus presenting a negative view of political leaders.

KEY FEATURES

Entman (1991) identifies five popular ways for framing news stories:

- *Conflict*: this focuses on disagreement and division, often within political parties. German Chancellor Schroeder suffered a famous dispute with his Deputy Oskar Lafontaine; equally the media tell us that UK Prime Minister Blair and Chancellor Gordon Brown are feuding over party leadership as well as a number of policies. Correspondingly, conflict between parties, especially in the US media, can be prioritised, as opposed to the actual decisions made.
- *Human Interest/Personalisation*: this introduces emotionalisation to news reporting and usually provides a story with a human face. Individual victims of natural disasters, wars or humanitarian crises are argued to have greater impact than facts and figures that are impossible to comprehend. While this can personalise politics by showing the effects of policy, it can also mean personality is promoted over other more important aspects.
- *Consequences*: while often focusing on economic ramifications of events (Semetko and Valkenburg, 2000), consequences can be wide ranging. Pursuing a policy may be unwise in terms of unity within a party or coalition or in terms of the status of a nation globally.
- *Morality*: media coverage can often moralise, sometimes due to the indiscretions of political actors; or alternatively, policies can be seen to be morally questionable. Michael Moore's editorialising of the US Patriot Act, the treatment of prisoners in Guantanamo Bay, as well as a number of worldwide critiques of US foreign policy all take a moral tone. Equally, there is a fight for the moral highground between pro-Palestinian and Israeli media coverage of their conflict.

political communication

83

- *Responsibility*: this frame attributes responsibility, either for a cause or a solution. In the wake of the Asian tsunami one frame was 'global responsibility' for finding solutions as well as blaming the lack of preparedness on the local governments.

These frames are defined as organising ideas or themes, ways of linking together stories historically, building up a narrative over time and across political space. Some of these frames can be used for specific types of event only, for example the reporting of the Asian tsunami was linked to consequences, how many further deaths there could be if aid was not received, and issues of responsibility. Other frames are more generic and could be used for any type of political news, for example conflict and the game of politics as opposed to frames that focus on values. It is also argued that news has become more personalised in an attempt to reach the postmodern audience, thus it cuts across reporting of disasters by introducing individual survivor's stories, news of politicians private lives. Even sports news can sometimes be seen to focus on a particular sportsperson's highs and lows rather than on their performance.

THE ACADEMIC AND PRACTICAL DEBATES

While it is argued that the frames act as heuristics, cognitive shortcuts, emerging from within the audience, that enable the easy processing of information, this is countered by arguments that information becomes oversimplified and distracts the public from the important issues. Each of the above frames are heavily criticised for their effect upon the audience, and their corresponding relations with and perceptions of the political system.

The emphasis on conflict, either within or between parties, individuals or organisations, is argued to induce public cynicism and lead to further disengagement from electoral politics. Personalisation is criticised for dumbing down political news and turning politicians into celebrities, others argue that politicians need to be humanised as this makes them appear relevant. However, when human interest is defined in terms of their private lives, and in particular, sexual indiscretions, this cannot encourage trust in the political system. The consequences frame is argued to contain much bias, for example Eurosceptic media coverage of European Monetary Union, or the European Constitution can lead to a negative perception of the European Union itself. The dominant frames in German, Dutch, Danish and UK media coverage of the euro are

key concepts

conflict and consequences, and some argue this directly influences the high levels of scepticism and was crucial for the Danish 'No' campaign (de Vreese et al., 2001).

In contrast, the morality and responsibility frames often betray the political bias of the media outlet. Poverty in developed nations can be framed as being the fault of the individual or the responsibility of the government. The rise of Muslim extremism can be blamed on US/UK policy in the Middle East, or these aspects can be ignored through a moral frame which makes extremism implicitly wrong. Thus framing is seen as necessary within media circles, but the dangers are often highlighted when democracy is mediated and most politics is communicated via mass media outlets.

FURTHER READING

For relevant works by Robert Entman, the foremost scholar on media framing, see R. Entman (1991) 'Framing US news: Contrasts in narratives of the KAL and Iran air incidents', *Journal of Communication*, 41 (4): 6–27; R. Entman (1993) and 'Framing: Towards a clarification of a fractured paradigm', *Journal of Communication*, 43 (4): 51–5. On audience framing and the audience reading of frames see V. Price, D. Tewkesbury and E. Powers (1997) 'Switching trains of thought: The impact of news frames on reader's cognitive responses', *Communication Research*, 24: 481–506. Examples of media framing are provided in H.A. Semetko and P.M. Valkenburg (2000) 'Framing European politics: A content analysis of press and television news', *Journal of Communication*, Spring: 93–109; C.H. de Vrees, J. Peter and H.A. Semetko (2001) 'Framing politics at the launch of the euro: a cross-national comparative study of frames in the news', *Political Communication*, 18: 107–22; D.A. Scheufele (1999) 'Framing as a theory of media effects', *Journal of Communication*, 49: 103–22.

Globalisation

> *Globalisation refers to the integration of the world's political, economic and media structures into a system where the nations are interdependent and interconnected through links visible and invisible, intended and accidental.*

ORIGINS AND LINKS

While originating in 19th century sociology, it was in the study of international relations during the 1960s and 1970s that the term emerged into common academic parlance. Since the collapse of the Soviet bloc, the trend towards integration has exacerbated through the information revolution. We now hear of the existence of a global information space we can all share; this is not only a physical entity, at our computer interface with the World Wide Web, but also less tangible, in the way we gather information and how media interact with our daily lives.

Clearly there are differing tiers of globalisation. On the one hand, there is political convergence towards a western democratic model, encouraged through state membership of multinational organisations such as the United Nations and the European Union. An example is Turkey's route to membership of the European Union, which has led to political reforms. There is also economic interdependence, with transnational corporations having branches across the globe and so relying on each national economy for their overall success or failure. Finally there is the information revolution; this allows the population of the world to move closer together, to be informed about, hear and see one another. These factors have all shaped modern political communication as political leaders and candidates no longer stand on just a national stage, but a global stage.

KEY FEATURES

In terms of political actors, their communication now has global reach and so they now think globally. This turns the well-voiced aphorism 'think global act local' on its head, for political leaders may speak locally but are heard globally. While related to international relations, the rhetoric of George W. Bush on foreign policy and global environmental agreements has worried some European leaders. Norwegian Prime Minister Kjell Bondevik, though one time leader of the 'No to the EU' campaign, argued that Bush's re-election in 2004 necessitates that European leaders co-operate more and speak 'in concert'. His comments were aimed at fellow European leaders, to indicate Norway was willing to take a more active role with the Union members; but also to Bush himself, suggesting he should take into account European political and public opinion prior to making policy decisions. While summits or high-profile meetings all serve similar functions in terms of communication, such events are more widespread and ordinary than is often considered. Bondevik, like many European leaders, is fully aware of the media attention such comments would earn and how they will be collected by global news corporations for dissemination.

The globalisation of the media is the second key feature. While politicians attempt to communicate on a global level, and are often successful at doing so via the media organisations, the media can have their own global agenda. Perhaps the best example of this is the independent Arab news station Al-Jazheera based in Qatar. Al-Jazheera reporters operated out of Baghdad throughout the 2002–3 Iraq War and presented a global audience with alternative views of the effects of the offensive. First, it was less sanitised and happily showed the atrocities caused by missiles fired into the Iraqi capital. Secondly, it acted as the voice of the Iraqi people, giving them a voice on the global stage that other news stations were either unable or unwilling to offer. The important role of Al-Jazheera was that it set the agenda for news stations in the US and the UK, the two main combatants. Al-Jazheera pictures were relayed to audiences across the globe by domestic media channels because a large percentage of the populations knew these alternative reports existed. To satisfy their audiences, they had to give Al-Jazheera airtime, thus offering news that was not 'restricted for security purposes', such as embedded journalists' reports, and that could be construed as unsupportive of the UK/US execution of the invasion.

THE ACADEMIC AND PRACTICAL DEBATES

While the case of Al-Jazheera may suggest that globalisation acts as a leveller in terms of pluralist power, many argue this is not the case. Studies of previous conflicts show that the powerful nations, with their attendant media management strategies, have redefined their public diplomacy to promote their own version of wars both domestically and internationally (Thussu, 2002). This, for the US and UK, is aided by the global reach of CNN and the BBC, which are given sole access, though controlled, and so are able to set the agenda for how the war is considered. While this is true, the example of Al-Jazheera illustrates the true levelling quality of globalisation, and that is that other outlets have access to a global audience. CNN found that they were not in control of the agenda during the Kosovo conflict because of the changes to the global public sphere. US journalist Carol Guensberg records that: 'Yugoslavia is a wired country . . . people are able to communicate directly in chat rooms with people in the conflict zone' (1999) and presents this as evidence for the emergence of a global community. Such arguments are relevant to the case of Al-Jazheera, as well as to some extent the Baghdad blogger whose words became a column in UK broadsheet the *Guardian*. Thus the arguments that globalisation reinforces styles of democracy and communication and so is a dominant discourse based upon existing inequalities (Walby, 2001) are not wholly accurate.

In terms of the media, Al-Jazheera notwithstanding, there is discussion of an internal conflict. On the one hand, there is the drive towards homogenisation of style of programming, while on the other, there are issues of domestication or localisation of news values (Clausen, 2004). This is argued not to allow the global public to converge in character or culture, but that the symbolic distance between communities, be they religious, racial or geographic, become accentuated and stereotypical. Images of the western world, offered by US programming popular in Russian and China, are highly selective and highlight the particularism of these nations and not the similarities between East and West. They may present images that are attractive, or ones that are abhorrent. Perhaps we can relate this to Huntingdon's clash of civilisations thesis, two worlds, the western and the Muslim, separated by perceptions based upon stereotypes. Such perceptual myths in theory should be removed due to the access offered by the globalisation of media access and coverage; however, many argue they remain powerful as a result of the global access, rather than being destroyed by its emergence.

FURTHER READING

On the globalisation of communication see Thompson's chapter in David Held and Anthony McGrew (2000) *The Global Transformations Reader*. Oxford: Polity. pp. 202–15. For critical accounts of the levelling qualities of globalisation see: Daya Kishab Thussu (2002) 'Managing the media in an era of round-the-clock news: Notes from India's first tele-war', *Journalism Studies*, 3 (2): 203–12; Sylvia Walby (2001) 'From community to coalition: The politics of recognition as the handmaiden of the politics of equality in an era of globalisation', *Theory, Culture and Society*, 18 (2–3): 113–35. For alternative views see Lisbeth Clausen (2004) 'Localising the global: "Domestication" processes in international news production', *Media, Culture and Society*, 26 (1): 25–44; Carol Guensberg (1999) 'Online access to the war zone', *American Journalism Review*, May; Jim Hall (2000) 'The first Web war: "Bad things happen in unimportant places"', *Journalism Studies*, 1 (3): 387–404.

Hegemonic Model

Hegemony is concerned with domination, and in communication that certain ideas are dominant over others. The hegemonic model of communication argues that the elite in society decide what ideas dominate in the public sphere. These can be grandiose narratives such as race-superiority, capitalism or even the nature of democracy; or notions of morality, the nature of family and other social norms.

ORIGINS AND LINKS

The concept of the hegemony of ideas has its origins in Marxist thought and was developed by Antonio Gramsci in his 1930s' critique of Mussolini's Italy (Gramsci, 1971). He argued that social elites, including the church, exercise social and cultural leadership, telling the people how to live, in order to maintain power over the economic, political and cultural aspects of the **public sphere**. From a Gramscian analysis there is a consensus on the role and power of government, the place of **civic culture** and limits to participation that amalgamate to denote **citizenship**. This would be implicit in any form of social education, formal or informal, propagated by the media and all channels of popular culture, and would establish social norms which the populace abide by in order to fit in. Thus society is underpinned by a single social consciousness, from which laws and norms flow, determining the way in which society operates from the most basic level.

KEY FEATURES

Every society is governed by a set of norms, these are inescapable. They relate to how people interact, what is lawful and what is not, and without them we would exist in what Thomas Hobbes described in his book on social theory, *Leviathan*, as a state of nature where life is 'nasty, brutish and short'. However, underpinning Gramscian logic is that social norms are set by a society's superstructure, the elite, and the base or masses just comply. This is not through means of direct coercion, but through a de-politicised authority: which would include law enforcement agencies, figures of authority (teachers, traffic wardens, judges and magistrates) as well as government officials. These are not party political but employed on behalf of society to uphold their norms, the question is can these norms be changed and are they changed by society or by elites.

THE ACADEMIC AND PRACTICAL DEBATES

Two key issues need to be raised to understand how the hegemonic model fits with postmodern society. First, there is the question of the location of the superstructure. While each national polity has sovereignty, this has been challenged by rules on a range of issues, an important area being human rights and freedoms. While these are set by people in an abstract and ideal form, they are translated into social norms that members of communities, such as the United Nations or the European Union, must abide by to retain the benefits of membership. Thus the linearity of top-down models seems to be far more complex than they were in the era of Marx or Gramsci.

Secondly, society is more diffuse and national borders are no longer closed to the infiltration of alternative ideas. Commentators have noted the evolution of Chinese society away from Maoist ideas to ones that embrace traditional Buddhist teachings as well as capitalist precepts, forcing governments in Beijing to adapt in order to remain relevant, particularly following the debacle of Tianamen Square on 4 June 1989. This diffuseness is accelerated with the widespread use of the Internet, meaning that members of different societies can share ideas and do not have to rely on domestic media for education or information and so alternative social norms can be introduced beneath the level of government.

These two features have led to an upwards elongation of the

superstructure as well as a levelling out of the information society and a global diffusion of civic society. Thus whether societies are moving to a point where all will conform to some global norm, founded on an ideal formed within elite communities or structures or shaped by human agency, is being debated. The impact on political communication is clear. Societies are no longer self-contained; we are able to read a range of globally-based media which can counter the hegemony of our own polities (consider the impact on western audiences of access to Al-Jazeera during the 2003 Iraq War and subsequent occupation). Furthermore, greater access to a range of information means we are not, automatically, forced to receive one single set of ideas and norms but can access a range of 'voices' offering alternatives: the culture of web-logging or 'blogging' being particularly pertinent. So far it is difficult to determine the extent of the impact of these factors on the state or its domestic political organisations; however, it is likely that the hegemonic model is currently in decline as a model for explaining the root of social norms.

FURTHER READING

A thorough, but highly readable, discussion of power relations is offered in S. Lukes (2005) *Power: A Radical View*. Basingstoke: Palgrave. For a discussion related to media and communication see J. Martin-Barbero (1993) *Communication, Culture and Hegemony: From the Media to Mediation*. London: Sage; a discussion more specific to political communication can be found in L. Phillips (1998) 'Hegemony and Political Discourse: The lasting impact of Thatcherism', *Sociology*, 32 (4): 847–67. For the concept of hegemony and its origins see Antonio Gramsci (1971) *Extracts from Prison Notebooks*. London: Lawrence and Wishart.

Ideology

Ideology represents a set of ideas and beliefs that act as both a guide and a constraint upon party and candidate behaviour. These ideas shape political outcomes in an attempt to change society to match an ideal.

ORIGINS AND LINKS

All religious or political ideals are ideological, from Catholicism and Protestantism, to conservatism or communism. Some ideologies are more prescriptive than others, so providing clearer guidance on behaviour. For example, socialism, theoretically, demands that the state own all means of production and share the wealth out among all members of the society. However, few socialist parties have adhered to this basic precept, and those that have did so using authoritarian means. Such historical instances lead us to question the extent to which ideology can actually offer political guidance, or whether it actually exists more in the form of an ethos; a guiding set of principles which suggest the kind of society a party or candidate aspires to while policy is created with a more pragmatic view.

The debates surrounding the role of political ideas suggest that **dealignment** and the rise of **electoral professionalism** have weakened attachments to ideology and that these are replaced with **consumerism**. Thus **political marketing** is argued to eschew ideology in favour of a more managerialist style of governing.

KEY FEATURES

In terms of political parties, ideology represents the core. It is the heart of the party, adherence to which binds its members and shapes its activities. Similar notions are used in branding theory, whereby any corporation will be guided not only by profit but by a set of principles: Body Shop and animal rights for example. The role of ideology is depicted in Figure 8 and shows the place of ideology in terms of values – that which a party stands for and is indivisible, such as liberalism, or equal opportunity for all – and ethos – which represents the psychological aspects: that being a member of the party suggests a shared perspective of society and how it should be shaped. The ideology is shared by the people, members, candidates and officers, and is represented in policies; so the outcome is known in terms of its effect on society. Ideology is then transmitted through communication on policy, symbols become iconic of the ideology and the image and ideology are naturally in tune with one another.

The communication will be designed to demonstrate how ideology has shaped policy and how the ideals that underpin the ethos and values will be realised through the direction the party or organisation is promoting. While much symbolic communication can be used by an ideological

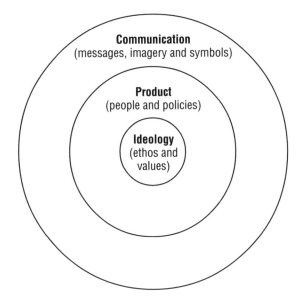

Figure 8   *The place of ideology in a party's brand*

party, they often also adopt an educationalist communication strategy. This, put simply, is designed to persuade the voter that this is the right course of action, based on the intended social outcomes, and that the party is able to put the policy into practice.

THE ACADEMIC AND PRACTICAL DEBATES

During the last decade of the 20th century, and partly in response to the collapse of communism, ideology was declared to be dead (Fukuyama, 1992). The debate on professionalisation and Americanisation, and political marketing, equally highlights the prioritisation of a managerialist approach to government backed by the packaging of communication into media-friendly messages that are designed to appeal to short-term needs of the voter rather than aspiring to deliver a better society long-term. Where ideological references are made, they are often seen as vague and reinforcing a pragmatic approach to governance: particularly we can highlight references to the Third Way by leftist political leaders during the 1990s such as German Chancellor Shroeder's *Die Neue Mitte* or US President Clinton's New Democrat strategy.

   Evidence, however, suggests that references to ideology remain important. George W Bush campaigned on a compassionate conservative platform in 2002, UK Conservative leader Michael Howard affirmed his credo in a press release of 2003, while New Zealand Labour leader Helen Clark offered pledge cards that explicitly combined voters' most important problems with traditional party values. The latter is a good example of the continued role of ideology. In turning social issues identified through market research into policies, the outcomes are often shaped with reference to the values and ethos of a party. This allows differentiation between candidates and voters to form attachments, if only for specific electoral contests. A study in the UK found working-class voters may not see themselves as loyal Labour voters, but that they see that party as offering more to them because of their belief that the party is on the left of the political spectrum (Lilleker, 2002). The problem in the UK is that the Labour Party is becoming less and less identified as having an ideological core and so is losing the trust of voters (Lilleker, 2005). This may well highlight the future importance of ideology as remaining at the core of the party to aid identification, in the same way that a management team will be chosen because it will uphold the values of an organisation.

FURTHER READING

On the end of ideology see F. Fukuyama (1992) *The End of History and the Last Man*. Harmondsworth: Penguin; for debates see D. Weltman and M. Billig (2001) 'The political psychology of contemporary anti-politics: A discursive approach to the end-of-ideology era', *Political Psychology*, 22 (2): 367–82. Sceptical views of the Third Way and the updating of ideology are introduced in A. Callinocos (2002) *The Third Way and its Dissenters*. London: Sage, albeit from a Marxist perspective. For a study in the UK which demonstrates the existent need for ideology see D.G. Lilleker (2002) 'Whose left? Working-class political allegiances in post-industrial Britain', *International Review of Social History*, 47: 65–85, and for one that highlights the danger of allowing ideology to become vague see D.G. Lilleker 'Political marketing: The cause of a democratic deficit?', *Journal of Non-profit and Public Sector Marketing*, 14 (1): 1–23.

Image

Image is the outward representation of a political leader, candidate or organisation. It is largely a construct that exists in the mind, but is based on the audience's power to decode the way that those individuals or organisations behave, combined with what audience members take from the way those individuals or organisations have been portrayed in the media and the manner and style in which they communicate.

ORIGIN AND LINKS

With the rise of television as the main medium of communication, and the shrinking coverage of political campaigns, and political activity in general, it became necessary for political communicators to transmit a lot of material in a short time. Central to this is image, and what elements are key for the postmodern audience. Thus much attention is devoted to image construction and communication, and it is central to the professionalised and marketised political communication context of the current era. A recent study of the mediation of politicians' image, taking in 17 countries, found that the phenomenon of highly stylised candidates, setting themselves up as self-made men or women who have overcome personal adversity, are family-oriented and possess a range of **authentic** values which inform political principles is global (Stanyer and Wring, 2004: 3).

Thus in the modern age of campaigning, we find politics becoming **celebritised** and a greater focus made of personalities. This promotes the **emotionalisation** of politics, **campaigns** attempting to promote a candidate's authenticity and the individual rather than the political; and sees **popular culture** invading the political sphere.

KEY FEATURES

The promotion of image by politicians is motivated first by widescale public disengagement from politics, and secondly by the media focusing on celebrity and personality. To reach the public psychologically, and to find media space, politicians have begun to promote aspects of their character that would usually be seen to be private and irrelevant. Thus the birth of Leo Blair became big news as the proud father, UK Prime Minister Tony Blair, paraded his new born son in front of the Downing Street press corps. Similarly in Britain, the loss of Chancellor Gordon Brown's first baby and subsequent birth of son John, became big news stories, both of which contributed to an emotionalisation of the dour, bookish accountant-like figure as Brown was previously characterised.

The global reach of such trends is highlighted by examples from Indian politics, where the cast of TV epic *Ramayana* appeared at rallies organised by the Congress Party and politicians compete for space on page 3 of the *Times of India* city supplements by appearing at product launches, fashion shows and rubbing shoulders with Bollywood stars and associated glitterati. This is argued to effect public perceptions of politicians, and indeed the purpose of political communication itself. Equally, the self-promotional activities of Chuwit Kamolvisit, leader of Thailand's Chat Thai or National Party, elevated the party to third place at the 2005 election, an unprecedented leap from being an outsider in electoral politics.

THE ACADEMIC AND PRACTICAL DEBATES

In essence, political communication should be designed to inform the public, about the organisation, candidates, leaders, and aid voters to decide how to vote or whether to offer active support. However, if the focus is purely image, it is argued that the decisions are founded purely on the ephemeral as opposed to the substance. While the effect is difficult to quantify, voters in the UK and US have replied to surveys that image is important: usually between 30–40 per cent. The media focus on politicians' private lives, however, particularly if there is a whiff of scandal, is argued to devalue politics as infotainment. Though this is debated in terms of it raising interest, one must ask if it is the right interest in the right aspects that is being encouraged.

A further area of debate is the element of credibility. While deference in politicians and in authority figures in general is far weaker now than in previous decades, there are questions regarding whether image-conscious politicians are taken seriously. In an Indian context, Mukherjee (2004, in Stanyer and Wring) argues that respect, couched in terms of deference, is in decline. This is noted by other contributors too (Stanyer and Wring, 2004), and is seen as a result of the celebritisation of politics and dumbing down of political news coverage. This raises an interesting problem for political communication: politics is seen to lack relevance and political actors as being out of touch with the people; however, because such issues are largely perceptual, politicians can make efforts to alter this image. The problem is that when they do they run the risk of undermining the political skills for which they seek to gain greater respect. Currently there are few tenable solutions to this important quandary, particularly as there are various perspectives of the results of the current tools employed to improve the image of politics.

FURTHER READING

On image politics see J. Street (2004) 'Celebrity politicians: Popular culture and political representation', *British Journal of Politics and International Relations*, 6 (4): 435–52. A review of global trends in the media reporting of image politics can be seen in James Stanyer and Dominic Wring (2004) 'Public images, private lives: The mediation of politicians around the globe', *Parliamentary Affairs*, 57 (1).

Information Subsidies

> *An information subsidy is information provided to a newsroom directly from a source in order to gain access to the media and earn time and space.*

ORIGINS AND LINKS

Gandy (1982), referring to the nature of the power relations between sources and journalists, coined the phrase information subsidy. It is accepted that the former needs coverage and the latter copy, particularly in a 24/7 news environment with ever tightening deadlines. The new media environment is argued to have given the source greater control over the news agenda: by developing a relationship built on trust with the reporter they can have open and ready access to the media audience. However, ready access relies on the news editor's decision based on perceptions of the credibility of the source, their relevance to the media audience and the interest of the information subsidy.

KEY FEATURES

While much academic attention focuses on the last vestiges of press–party parallelism in the US and Russia, and the breakdown in source–reporter relations in the UK, France and Germany, different tiers of the political structure have differing qualities of relations with the media. The arena where the majority of information subsidies are successful is between local political organisations and the media. Local media news values are quite simply localised, tend not to have a political axe to grind, are more focused on providing what their audiences want from the local media, and lack the resources for celebrity scoops – any gossip they get is usually second-hand. Therefore they offer access to any organisation that can fit the editorial criteria.

Political communicators and electoral consultants stress making national politics local; this makes the local media a key publicity vehicle. However, politicians find that the agenda is largely set by the local media, and that they can refuse to cover political events, including elections, on a whim. It is within this context that many liberal democracies operate: where political communication is reduced to soundbites and the media largely control what information is allowed to enter the public sphere.

THE ACADEMIC AND PRACTICAL DEBATES

Though the media still have power as a gatekeeper, excluding that which is deemed inaccurate, not newsworthy or uninteresting to the audience, the extent of their power in this area is questioned. However, discussions of the importance of media news values, their power over the news agenda, and political accounts of being unable to control the way that political statements are delivered to the audience suggest the reverse is the case. We could assume that accounts of media power on the one hand, and those of media management strategies on the other, lead to a situation of reasonable parity. Power is fragmented and disparate.

Studying accounts of journalists, political editors, politicians and their communications strategists it appears that they largely lack any understanding of one another, which is curious considering the degree of interaction and crossover that exists in many western democracies. The media seeks to break a story and then add detail, including alternative perspectives and opinions, until the story begins to lose public interest. The market orientation of the media means they seek to provide their audience with what they want, and that is not always objective political policy information. Therefore politicians must follow the media agendas when launching stories for public consumption. While media management may work, political editors receive masses of material, which means that it is rare for stories to reach the news in an unadulterated form.

FURTHER READING

An excellent introduction is provided in Oscar H. Gandy (1982) *Beyond Agenda Setting: Information Subsidies and Public Policy*. Norwood, NJ: Ablex). On media relations see Jean Seaton (ed.) (1998) *Politics and the Media*. Oxford: Blackwell; on the workings of the media see Stuart Allen (1999) *News Culture*. Buckingham: Open University Press.

Infotainment

> *A constructed noun, infotainment is the combination of the words information and entertainment, suggesting a practice of the blending together of their presentation within the broadcasting of news and current affairs.*

ORIGINS AND LINKS

Infotainment describes the way in which the modern mass audience largely receives political communication. It is argued that, with the disengagement of the public from 'hard' news due to the fragmentation of mass media, politicians will communicate in more entertaining, media-friendly, ways, while the news media will make news more entertaining and reflective of popular culture. As Maurice Edelman (1995: 1) argues, political communication becomes situated in **frames** that belong to other popular genres like 'novels, paintings, stories, films, dramas, television sitcoms, striking rumours, even memorable jokes'.

While not fundamentally new (as far back as the 1920s Walter Lippmann discussed the use of sensationalism in news coverage and political discourse), recent social changes, technological advances and the market orientation of the mass media have led increasingly to political information being transmitted via non-traditional channels. To some this is increasing the relevance and **authenticity** of politics; to others it causes the **dumbing down** of political communication and media **news values**.

KEY FEATURES

There are two key features, one relating to the behaviour of politicians, the other to the media. Politicians may attempt to meld themselves into popular culture, for example the appearances on chat shows of UK Prime Minister Blair, US President Clinton or French URP leader Nicolas Sarkozy. Using existing popular culture they will attempt to offer alternative perceptions of themselves: UK Liberal Democrat leader Charles Kennedy is to make a cameo appearance in top-rated soap opera *EastEnders*, other UK politicians have appeared on the satirical news quiz *Have I Got News For You*; elsewhere politicians may borrow the services of celebrities to appear in campaign advertisements, which may also be designed with popular culture in mind. Thus we find politicians trying to communicate aspects of their image, style and policy, through appearances within popular culture, or using formats of communication that mirror popular culture.

The media, meanwhile, can package news in an entertaining way. This, to some extent, can be the news frame: divisions within the political elite, scandals, sexual impropriety, the horse race reportage of elections all attempt to gain viewers for news programmes while fulfilling the media role of information provider. Thus we find not just tabloid newspapers, but all media channels running stories on UK Home Secretary David Blunkett's affair with a married woman, a story that spiralled out of control as the revelations stacked up. Similarly the fall of Gerhard Glogowski, 'a close ally of German Chancellor Gerhard Schroeder', became a soap opera within news reports, while the trial and subsequent sentencing of former French Prime Minister Alain Juppe became an indictment on President Chirac, so building the level of suspense and intrigue common with courtroom dramas and thrillers. While all these stories are news, and it is important that they are placed into the public sphere, commentators question the sensationalisation and its impact on civic culture and, perhaps, its contribution to public cynicism.

THE ACADEMIC AND PRACTICAL DEBATES

The study by Delli Carpini and Williams (2001) sees both positives and negatives in recent trends. An important positive is that with the collapse of divisions between news and entertainment within the new media environment, power over information is removed from the political elite. While they employ sophisticated news management strategies, the agendas are increasingly set by journalists. They will decide what is, and is not, newsworthy, and will pursue the stories they believe to be in the public interest or more often of interest to the public. Hence politics is no longer a closed world run by self-serving elites; they have to be far more accountable and, as the cases of Blunkett, Glogowski and Juppe indicate, will be brought to account for wrongdoings.

While this is true, it is questioned whether this leads to a cynical perspective of politics, that it is the cause for the lack of trust in our political leaders. Due to the sensationalisation of such events, and Delli Carpini and Williams (2001) focus on the Clinton–Lewinsky affair, actual damage can be caused to the public's relationship with politicians. The building of a story into an epic of intrigue, love, lust, betrayal, all the features of a Hollywood blockbuster, means that all that is political and actually matters to the running of society is actually sidelined.

This is also related to the way in which politicians package themselves. Franklin's argument that politics is not the same as soap, an age-old adage, is highly pertinent (2004). Critics ask should politicians appear, or feel the need to appear, in soap operas, or on popular television shows, and does this contribute to the disengagement as politicians are no longer taken seriously. It could be argued that the modern political consumer wants to see the human, emotional, real character of the political leader, and that using popular culture enables other aspects of the character to be communicated. In fact, research in the USA has shown that voters with lower education, who are disengaged from a campaign, will use the appearances of candidates on chat shows to inform their voter choice (Baum, 2005). Partially, this is a basis for some commentators to worry that the line between fact and fiction is becoming blurred, that as politicians appear as actors or celebrities and political stories are played out under dramatic headlines, politics is reduced to being a tawdry soap opera with too many characters, too few events and little of interest to a public with a plethora of choices of entertainment. Voter cues become derived from the ephemera, which could allow the election of good performers but bad politicians; a feature of the Austrian election that saw Jorge Haider gain power perhaps.

FURTHER READING

Murray Edelman (1995) *From Art to Politics*. Chicago: University of Chicago Press, remains a seminal study. For a more recent study from the US see Delli Carpini and Williams (2001) 'Let us infotain you: Politics in the new media environment', in W. Lance Bennett and Robert M. Entman, *Mediated Politics: Communication in the Future of Democracy*. New York: Cambridge University Press. pp. 160–81. A critical account from the UK perspective is in Bob Franklin (2004) *Packaging Politics*. London: Arnold; this is contrasted in M.A. Baum (2005) 'Talking the vote: Why presidential candidates hit the talk show circuit', *American Journal of Political Science*, 49 (2): 213–41.

Legitimacy/ Legitimisation

Legitimacy describes the wielding of power legally as accepted by all members of the society; hence it is a quality that all political structures should be seen to have within democratic nations. It is founded on the belief that they derive their power from the public and so act only in the name of that public. Political communication, used to persuade the public that a policy is correct, or used to interact with the public regarding policy options, can offer further legitimisation to any group that wields power.

Power is demonstrated in a number of ways through action and communication. Through the legal system, governments wield their power on a daily basis; they also use communication and the flow of information as a way of managing their retention of power. However, a number of other organisations wield power within a democratic society, their power being derived from those they represent. A corporate group or cartel, for example, are argued to be more powerful due to the economic status of their members. Other pressure groups demonstrate their power through assembling their members on the streets to show support for their argument: such as the global movement against the war in Iraq. Equally, terrorist groups can display their power through direct action. What separates these groups is the degree of legitimacy each can claim to possess, and their perceived legitimacy in the eyes of the publics they communicate to and with. Some may argue that organisations like the Organisation of Petroleum Exporting Countries (OPEC) are nothing more than economic terrorists due to their control over the world's oil reserves; similar claims could be made against many economic cartels. Others may argue that the direct and often shocking demonstrations of power by pressure or terrorist groups are legitimate because they are excluded from other methods of communication. Hence the debates surrounding legitimacy and who holds the legitimate right to wield power are as old as debates on democracy itself, and each person may well have an opposing view of what is legitimate.

Democratic theorist Robert Dahl (1961) likened democracy to a reservoir, arguing that if there is insufficient legitimacy then the state or organisation becomes unstable. This can be due to the perceived unlawful use of power, or feeling that another group possesses greater representative legitimacy. In both cases it is suggested that legitimacy will dry up and when that happens that the state or leadership be replaced by another body. At the heart of this debate is the question of how political communication can contribute to legitimisation. If communication is simply produced to persuade then clearly we cannot base legitimacy purely on coercion. Thus many of the debates on the importance of style and image can lead to a debate on the extent to which such **political communication**, and the voter choices it produces, contributes to the legitimacy of a political system. Equally, the way in which information is presented, or indeed how much information is imparted, can suggest how legitimately power is exercised.

political communication

103

Clearly not every political organisation can use communication tools to legitimise itself. While we may agree with the cause that certain groups stand for, that does not in essence mean they are legitimate. This is highlighted by various studies of the European Union that query in spite of the fact that it is recognised as an official entity – there are members elected to its parliament and a proportion of European citizens' taxes contribute to its upkeep – whether it has any legitimate power. While the answer is yes, under international law, many European citizens have formed parties and organisations to argue that it has no legitimate power; this is a perception that Meyer (1999) argues can be overcome through successful communication. The dimensions, or elements of an organisation, Meyer argues should be communicated are broadened out here to suggest a model that can be applied to any political organisation.

First, are the issues. Too often it appears that policy is determined behind closed doors, out of the public gaze, and follows procedures that are neither explained nor tangible. Clearly some issues are made public, through or by the media before they are a fait accompli. The majority, however, remain hidden. Meyer (1999) argues that information on the issues that are being debated within an organisation need to be shared broadly, with the mass public or perhaps at least among an organisation's membership. There seems to be an increasing demand that the public as well as any organisation's key stakeholders are included and is able to have input, suggesting that legitimacy necessitates a two-way model of communication.

Secondly, and expanding on the argument on the communication of issues, is the question of making procedure open. It can relate to informing at what stage one particular issue is on the decision-making ladder, alternatively it can suggest that procedures should be open and accountable. Particularly important is what points of access exist for the public or members to have a say.

Thirdly, communication needs to stress the accountability of individuals, groups, departments or tiers of an organisation for any particular policy, in terms of both its origin and any measurement of success or failure. An example of this can be offered through a discussion of the different communication processes of some online pressure groups and political parties. The latter have a range of working groups that conduct research, debate and discuss options and then set policy. While the leader may well be seen as accountable overall for the policy, it is less clear how others are involved, and when failure of an initiative becomes public then blame can sometimes be apportioned elsewhere. Some pressure groups use discussion boards on the World Wide Web to determine policy: suggestions will be posted from anyone signed up, the debate will occur between contributors and a decision will be made. While all are accountable, the process is clear and in-fighting cannot break out over the apportioning of blame.

Meyer (1999) notes that this prioritises communication to a position at the heart of any organisation that seeks to claim legitimacy. This means, explicitly, that all members of an organisation will become responsible for engaging in some form of communication or another. It also suggests that the majority of communication has to be two-way, in terms of the public not only asking questions and gaining responses, but also having some input into decision making.

THE ACADEMIC AND PRACTICAL DEBATES

The above argument may appear to conflate legitimacy with transparency: that if an organisation is open and inclusive then it will be perceived as legitimate. While perhaps this is not far from the truth, it does not overcome the problem of perceptions being far from universal. Some would argue that legitimacy is based on the number of supporters, asking 'in whose name do you speak' before deciding whether to listen or not. While such a question could be asked of any organisation, including the supranational United Nations or European Union, it is more likely to be used against pressure groups when lobbying their opponents or the unsympathetic. This can particularly be the case if the media does decide such a group is newsworthy. If we consider the way that Greenpeace, animal rights groups, separatist groups or consumer rights organisations can be treated either identically or in vastly different ways, we gain an insight into the way that the media can offer legitimacy to a group or can de-legitimise the group and its argument.

The role of the media in giving voice to political organisations, as well as then mediating and editorialising their outputs, has changed the nature of campaign communication. This does not just apply to the electoral parties; it has also affected the way in which a variety of differing groups communicate. They often are forced to play to the symbolic to appear legitimate, to use spin and image management, and so can fail to meet the standards set by Meyer (1999). For some organisations this may necessitate legitimising themselves to a virtual community and resorting to e-politics apart, of course, from those times when direct action is required. On the other hand, those organisations that have to remain in

the eye of the mass public may be compelled to develop news management strategies in order to get their message across; unfortunately this may not help the public perception of their legitimacy.

FURTHER READING

A good introduction to the concept of legitimacy can be found in M.S. Weatherford (1992) 'Measuring political legitimacy', *American Political Science Review*, 86: 187–205; see also R. Dahl (1961) *Who Governs?* New Haven, CT: Yale University Press. For a debate on the role of communication in the legitimisation of political organisations, from the perspective of a study into the European Union see C. Meyer (1999) 'Political legitimacy and the invisibility of politics: Exploring the European Union's communication deficit', *Journal of Common Market Studies*, 37 (4): 617–39. For a debate on legitimacy of political groups and the role of the media see B. Szerszynski (2003) 'Marked bodies: Environmental activism and political semiotics', in J. Corner and D. Pels, *Media and the Restyling of Politics*. London: Sage.

– Manufactured Consent –

The manufactured consent thesis argues that, as opposed to devotion to civic duty, democracies achieve harmony and consensus through manipulation of the people by the skilful use of the media and messages.

key concepts

ORIGINS AND LINKS

The phrase the 'manufacture of consent' was coined by Walter Lippman in 1922 (Lippman, 1997). This built on notions of the use of propaganda in a democracy and argued that consent for a policy was created through the deployment of 'necessary illusions'; that political leaders present a case in order to ensure there is little disagreement that cannot be regarded as extremist. This sharply contrasts with the idea of civic society, where the people consent to the will of the government on the basis that it acts as their elected representative.

Herman and Chomsky (1988) developed the concept further when they argued that the more democratic and open a society is, and the more educated and politically aware its people, then the more sophisticated and developed its 'thought control and indoctrination will be' (p. 2). Therefore, despite debates to the contrary, Chomsky and other academics insist that many of the developments in political communication are geared more at persuasion than at representation. Thus concepts such as **political marketing**, the emphasis on **style**, **aestheticisation** or **emotionalisation**, are seen as merely part of the methodology designed to manufacture public consent.

KEY FEATURES

Herman and Chomsky's study argues that political communication is dominated by the propagandist model (1988). This places the media as a subservient actor, simply communicating to the public a series of symbols and messages designed to entertain, amuse or inform. It is argued that there is hegemony over ideas and power rests in the hands of a small elite group, a 'specialised class' whose primary objective is to retain power.

Herman and Chomsky (1988) lay out a schemata to enable the reader to compare the communication they face with the propaganda model and the extent to which free access to objective information is permitted. They argue that there are five filters that determine which messages are relayed to the audience, and which are halted by the gatekeepers. They define these filters as:

1 Size, ownership and profit orientation of the mass media. It is argued that news values can be set by an elite group of news gatherers, such as Associated Press, AOL Time Warner or Reuters, who then filter news down the supply chain to their subsidiaries. This can keep some news management strategists or their stories on the margins, and out of the public sphere.

2 The advertising or sponsorship deals that support news production. Economic interest can mean that some issues are not raised, that some media companies with particular political bias can go out of business and that the media fall into the hands of an elite group – this is certainly Chomsky's view of news media in the USA.

3 Sourcing of news and reliance on elites. Pluralism can suffer as a result of reliance on a small corps of experts, news sources or recognised

political communication

briefs. Experts, whom sociologist Stuart Hall et al. (1978) referred to as the 'primary definers' within a society, may well be government officials who must support the official message; equally governments may attempt to control the flow of information through offering exclusives in return for control of the agenda. The media complicity in this is argued to enforce the hegemony of ideas.

4   Flak: selection of news and the attachment of bias. Flak is a term used by Herman and Chomsky to cover any attempts to undermine voices, from within the media or outside, that criticise the 'official' line. This was used to good effect within the US and UK media to criticise the UN, France and a number of media organisations and anti-war groups that opposed the 2003 Iraq War. US President Bush and UK Prime Minister Blair's references to the peace marchers as misguided and uninformed, as well as dangerous to the safety of the nation, are good examples of the practice.

5   Herman and Chomsky's fifth filter was anti-communism, defined as a national religion and control mechanism. Though this is now a feature of history, enemies still exist, or have been established, that fill that gap. George W. Bush's 'rogue states', the 'war on terror' or 'coalition of the willing' are all loaded phrases designed to create an 'us' and a 'them'. The media would respond by including themselves, and the public, as 'us'; disbarring supporters of 'them' from gaining unmediated, and so unqualified, access to the public.

Herman and Chomsky's work on media reporting and government communication in the USA found that such filters were often used by both spheres and, when used by government spokespersons, were usually reflected in subsequent media coverage. This led them to argue that the hegemonic alliance of government and media followed a propagandist communication model, limiting pluralism on key issues, particularly those on foreign policy, and ensuring that dissent was filtered out as a dangerous irrelevance or silenced completely.

THE ACADEMIC AND PRACTICAL DEBATES

Herman and Chomsky's core argument is that the media and government are complicit in subsidising the information entering the public sphere; going as far as to argue that the media will not cover a story that is not in the interests of the 'owners' of a country (1988). Owners would include the corporate giants, political leaders and media moguls, which they observe to often be the same people within a US context. And it is surrounding this notion of the context that we need to raise the core question regarding Herman and Chomsky's thesis: is this a purely US problem or one that is a global issue? O'Shaughnessy (2004) sees parallels between the governmental use of propaganda in the US and UK; though few argue that the UK media was as complicit in promoting the 2003 Iraq War, in fact the opposite was the case for many UK tabloids, broadsheets and news organisations. Taking a more global perspective it is possible to see elements of Chomsky's argument to be proven by a range of media news coverage during certain times. While, normally, war is a time when media and government talk with a unitary voice, and that dissent is often pushed to the margins, this is not always the case in the everyday coverage of politics: not even in the USA.

Does this mean that Chomsky's arguments are only valid within a US wartime context; the answer is not always. Does it mean that the manufacture of consent only occurs at times of national crisis; that is a far stronger argument. As O'Shaughnessy's study of propaganda shows, propaganda is more likely to be used when there is a perceived national threat, whether from within or from an external force (2004). Terrorism, war and economic disaster are all met with strong action, actual and verbal. But is this necessarily right? Any governmental leader would probably argue that in times of national crisis, popular consent and consensus are a must. If the nation is internally divided then mounting any sort of military or economic campaign is at least hindered. Historically this is because the war effort has begun at home; however, in the modern age the mass public see warfare as a televisual spectacle and barely feel any detrimental effects. As Michael Ignatieff (2004) noted in his critique of the **mediatisation** of modern warfare, the public are spectators of a virtual war, with cameras tracking missiles all the way to their targets and embedded journalists relaying images back to audiences from the front line. This sanitised reportage promotes a gung-ho pro-war attitude. It is argued that the concept of manufacturing consent is outdated, that honest and objective information should be sufficient to present a government's case. That this is not the case is worrying to many critics of the public relations democracy.

The latter contradiction raises further questions. An important question being has the introduction of public relations and marketing to government increased the manufacture of consent? Some would argue that the 'smoke and mirrors' that are used by government communication experts hinder our understanding of the facts and instead promote begrudging acceptance. Others argue that spin is more likely to promote cynicism and, as such, is self-defeating. Thus the extent to which attempts

political communication

are made to manufacture public consent is open to interpretation, both in practical terms and surrounding its effects.

FURTHER READING

The classic text is Herman and Chomsky (1988) *Manufacturing Consent*. London: Vintage; See also Walter Lippman (1997) *Public Opinion*. New York: Free Press where the phrase 'manufacture of consent' was first introduced. See also Michael Ignatieff (2004) *Virtual War*. New York: Picador. On the history of propaganda see N. O'Shaughnessy (2004) *Politics and Propaganda: Weapons of Mass Seduction*. Manchester: Manchester University Press. A negative view of modern communication techniques is offered in J. Palmer (2002) 'Smoke and mirrors: is that the way it is? Themes in political marketing', *Media, Culture and Society*, 24: 345–63. See also S. Hall, C. Critcher, T. Jefferson, J. Clarke and B. Roberts (1978) *Policing the Crisis*. London: Macmillan.

Media-Centred Democracy

A media-centred democracy is a political system where a vast majority of political activity is conducted with the media in mind and that the public receive the vast majority of their information from media reporting.

110

ORIGINS AND LINKS

The term was coined by Donald Swanson and can be interchanged with a range of other terms employed to describe the centrality of media management to modern political communication. A media-centred democracy could also be described as a **public relations state**, and key to communication would be associated concepts such as designer politics,

political marketing communication and **mediatisation**. Commonly it is associated with the **Americanisation** thesis, that it is the Americanisation or **professionalisation** that recognises the communicative importance of the media, and particularly television, within postmodern society, and thus political communications must adapt to this. While it is usual to illustrate political communication as being semi-mediated, it is argued that this is changing. With less activity taking place at the interpersonal level, and the inability to reach a critical mass of voters through traditional face-to-face events or via new media, the mass media remains the key mode for reaching a mass audience. Television can allow political actors to interact with the public, often through debates with studio audiences or interviewers, and gives the public access to the person, but within the restrictions of the media logic.

KEY FEATURES

What features would we expect to see in a media-centred democracy? The fact is that most of us all live in such a system, it has steadily evolved over the last four decades, and hence we do not note massive shifts in behaviour. However, when applying such concepts to other nations, it is useful to set up benchmarks for comparing the extent of media-centredness. Key features therefore would be:

- A lack of face-to-face, local political activity apart from during election campaigns in key regions. This is exacerbated by having a mass electorate that is difficult to reach using other media: consider just in terms of size the USA, Russia or even France and Germany.
- The majority of funding will be devoted to television advertising (where regulation permits) or mass advertising and communication methods: across Europe, billboards are seen as useful to counter the lack of access to paid-for advertising: the staple of the US election campaign.
- Television will be used for maximum exposure, particularly using non-traditional forums: French party leader Sarkozy's use of chat shows mirrors a model employed successfully by a number of 'charismatic leaders' such as US President Bill Clinton, Italian Prime Minister Silvio Berlusconi and Russian President Vladimir Putin.
- Appearance and presentation, issues of image projection, will be prioritised above delivering political messages. The celebritisation leads politicians to try to humanise themselves by using every opportunity to stake out their political territory.

political communication

Media-Centred Democracy

- Leaders and spokespersons may be chosen for their televisual skills and telegenic features, an area where increasingly training will be provided by parties, and media skills become central to the job specification of a party leader.
- Media coverage is seen as a goal in itself, media management will become a central feature of party campaigning: this is evidenced by the widespread use of rapid rebuttal systems such as the UK Labour Party's Excalibur computer.
- Communication professionals will have a greater role in party campaigning, as is seen by the virtually global phenomenon of the campaign consultant and spin-doctor.

While these features can be central to any democracy, most are expected to be associated with a completely free press, something that is not always present in a democracy. While press/media freedom can always be debated, if the media is under some form of state control some aspects, such as rapid rebuttal, would be less necessary. However, as noted in Hallin and Mancini (2004), the level of convergence across the globe is leading to a homogenisation of media systems and hence the media strategy of the political actors.

THE ACADEMIC AND PRACTICAL DEBATES

Clearly it is questionable whether so much effort and expenditure should be put into what is arguably a peripheral aspect of politics: the communication of image. However, as politicians increasingly have to compete with corporate marketing communication for public attention, and with celebrities lifestyles for media coverage, it is evident there is a need to adapt to news values and media agendas and become 'media savvy'. The latter is widely described as understanding the media, offering the media what they want and fitting to media paradigms; it is not believing that just because one is a political figure one is naturally newsworthy. Therefore political actors must play the media game. However, it is argued that the prioritisation of media management does democratic politics a disservice and that designer politics causes a dumbing down of the political debate by distracting public attention from that which is important, thus trivialising the organisations that run society. Thus we find politicians in a catch-22 situation, either dumbed down or ignored.

Accordingly, it is towards the media that much criticism is directed. Ratuva (2003) argues that the media is seldom an 'autonomous, objective, innocent entity with a god's eye view of the world', rather he describes the various media outlets as struggling to maintain their economic survival. It is this struggle that journalists argue forces the media to editorialise, to be subjective and biased, to take a political stance based on the perceived stance of the readership. However, the biasing of reporting can give readers a narrow, skewed view of the world, arguably encouraging media malaise and voter disengagement. This is certainly Ratuva's perspective when he argues 'the power of the pen can be used to inflame conflict, create goodness, undermine political power, distort reality and invent truth' (2003); it is the negatives that in his view are promoted most often by the mass media.

The media's power to determine news values, to promote frames that make politics appear trivial, or at worst corrupt, means that a media-centred democracy may have high levels of public disengagement and a fracturing of the link between the public and their representatives. This is seen by some as a negative aspect of the increasing importance of the media, but by others such as Pippa Norris (2000) as the means by which politics is made interesting to a largely disinterested, postmodern media audience.

FURTHER READING

For the debate on media-centred democracy and its links to Americanisation see R. Negrine (1996) *The Communication of Politics*. London: Sage. pp. 146–66; 176–9. Global media systems, and the extent of homogenisation, is covered in D.C. Hallin and P. Mancini (2004) *Comparing Media Systems: Three Models of Media and Politics*. Cambridge: Cambridge University Press. A critical view of the media's role in a pluralist democracy is offered by S. Ratuva (2003) 'The politics of the media: a cynical synopsis', *Pacific Journalism Review*, 9: 177–81. Alternative views are offered in P. Norris (2000) *A Virtuous Circle*. London: Sage.

political communication

113

Media Effects

Media effects research studies the way in which media output, in this case the way that politics is reported to the audience, influences audience members in terms of perceptions, attitudes and behaviour. Thus, if the media are chief influencers, when a popular tabloid newspaper endorses a candidate the public should support them also; if they criticise a candidate or party the public should build a negative perception.

ORIGINS AND LINKS

Media effects theory has been around as long as academic interest in the mass media. The basic hypothesis is that because the public access the majority of their information in a mediated form then the way that that information is **packaged**, or **mediated**, must effect the audience members' attitudes and behaviour. On this basis various research studies have linked violence on the screen to violence in society, watching soap operas and suffering from mental anxiety, as well as negative reporting of politicians and public cynicism.

The most frequent discussions focus on the way that the media set **agendas** and **frame** news coverage, each of which has been claimed to have profound influence on media audiences. However, here we should also consider the use of media management strategies as these represent attempts to control media coverage in order to have a direct effect, from sender to receiver, through mediated communication.

KEY FEATURES

The evolution of media effects theory has seen a number of dominant, and often competing, academic perspectives come to the fore, each of which tries to explain empirically how the audience is affected by media outputs. Early effects theory used the metaphor of a hypodermic needle: that the media would offer a unitary discourse, for instance that communism is bad and, over time, we would accept that as the truth. The problem with this theory is that there are competing viewpoints and that exposure to these, as well as to the dominant, 'injected' discourse, means each audience member is able to make their own judgement. Similar arguments that there are other influences at work other than the media are developed to refute the power of framing. These argue, for example, that media coverage of the European Union in countries like Norway and the UK is not the sole reason for the organisation's negative perception by the public.

Agenda-setting theory is thus more tentative. It states that the media cannot instruct how to think, but it can encourage the audience to think about certain issues: spin, sleaze, the lack of choice in democracy, the divisions within a party, splits in a coalition, the lack of democracy in the European Union. However, do we always think about the things that the media want us to? Borrowing a popular theory from marketing communications, the Elaboration Likelihood Model argues that we must be interested in the issue in order to allow details to enter our subconscious. Audience members assess the relevance of a message, be it mediated or direct from a political party or candidate, within the subconscious where it is processed; is it understood or not, and a decision taken whether the message should be rejected. When it matches other peripheral cues we have received, or is accepted by our understanding of the context it relates to, the message can alter behaviour. However, the change is dependent on the audience member's willingness to listen, their ability to understand and the extent to which it is acceptable to them.

In contrast, however, just because we are not interested, or do not see the relevance in a message, does not mean it is not remembered. While not going full circle to reinvent the hypodermic effect, it is true that we absorb information from heuristics, mental shortcuts in the form of symbols or easily remembered phrases; just consider how many advertising slogans that you can remember despite having never bought the product or been even remotely interested in that product category. This is termed 'low attention processing', that by osmosis we absorb heuristics that inform our perspectives and perceptions of parties, candidates, organisations or systems. One example in the UK would be the current low opinion of politicians. Arguably this is fed to media audiences through a focus on private misdemeanours, particularly sexual infelicities; abuse of office, cash for questions or Home Secretary David Blunkett's provision of a passport for his mistress's nanny; or the pervasive use of spin to obfuscate and mislead. The narrative is reinforced through political drama, such as BBC TV's *The Project*, or mainstream entertainment, such as BBC TV's *Have I Got News For You*, *Spooks*, *My Dad's the*

political communication

115

Prime Minister, and thus audiences have a reality constructed for them of what politics is about.

This links well with Cultivation Theory (Signorielli and Morgan, 1990), which argues that culture is maintained by the media. While society sets its norms, values and traditions, these are upheld internally through symbolic reference, while advertised outside society through stereotypical images of society. Thus we find the 'western' or 'American Way' portrayed in a range of situation comedies, dramas and soap operas that enjoy worldwide successes. However, such theories do not accommodate change easily. While political communication is about altering and shifting attitudes and behaviour, as is the role of propaganda, such theories focus on reinforcing and embedding existing perspectives. Thus we find that political communication relies on a simplified repeat–remind, public relations led strategy that believes in the hypodermic needle metaphor. In other words, parties and candidates act as if they believe that if they say they are the best for the job, and that their opponents are rubbish, we will eventually accept that view. Some studies argue that this type of communication only works on those predisposed to believe the message, thus the media is argued to have little real effect that is long term but instead there are scattered, fragmented influences that affect people on a daily basis, many of which are mediated by other competing influences.

THE ACADEMIC AND PRACTICAL DEBATES

The key question is: Does the media have any real effect? Given that media audiences are highly selective of which information they 'process' and which they ignore, and that in this age of information overload we are bombarded with a range of messages for us to process, the media is one influence out of many. Some would argue that we simply eschew all things political as it is not seen as relevant. Others posit that actually we do seek information, following a **uses and gratifications** model, but that we mistrust the media and the politicians and so seek our information elsewhere. This introduces the role of interpersonal communication and socialisation, which experiments indicate to be of more importance than our decoding of media outputs.

The fact that experimental research underpins most theories of media or communication effects makes some proclaim their redundancy. Experiments are carried out in synthetic environments. While participants may be in a 'living-room' it is not their living-room, similarly they are told to watch the television, read the newspaper or chat to the other people therein. Hence, it is not a replication of real behaviour, as no accurate method of research can observe us without causing a research effect: that we behave differently when watched. Thus, while theoretically there is an effect, it is difficult to assess how and when it manifests itself, hence David Gauntlett (1998) argues we should instead ask why there should be an effect rather than assuming there is one and attempting to gauge how it is induced.

FURTHER READING

The work of Bryant and Zillman is very important in the field of media effects, and a good introduction can be found in J. Bryant and D. Zillman (1994) *Media Effects: Advances in Theory and Research*. New Jersey: Lawrence Erlbaum; for a more advanced analysis see J. Bryant and D. Zillman (1991) *Responding to the Screen*. New Jersey: Lawrence Erlbaum; N. Signorielli and M. Morgan (1990) *Cultivation Analysis: New Directions in Media Effects Research*. Newbury Park, CA: Sage); D. Gauntlett (1998), 'Ten things wrong with the Effects Model', in R. Dickinson, R. Harindranath and O. Linne, *Approaches to Audiences: A Reader*. London: Edward Arnold. Contrasting, non-media, effects are discussed in E. Keller and J. Berry (2003) *The Influentials*. New York: Free Press; S. Lenart (1994) *Shaping Political Attitudes*. London: Sage.

Mediatisation

Mediatisation is a theory which argues that it is the media which shapes and frames the processes and discourse of political communication as well as the society in which that communication takes place.

political communication

ORIGINS AND LINKS

The public sphere is argued to be founded on 'well-informed communication', but for this to be the case all the relevant facts and argumentation need to be made available and accessible to the public (Thompson, 1990). While in many pluralist democracies this is the case, for example the principle of open government in the UK has made a raft of documentation available from governmental department websites, the fact that few people access that information is indicative of modern society. Largely the **public sphere** is informed by the media, thus information is mediatised as all coverage can suffer from the media outlet's attendant bias and **framing** and must be located within media **agendas** and conform to established **news values**.

Studies of where political information is obtained have a long pedigree, for example as long ago as 1969 in the UK and 1970 in the US they found that the former relied mainly on radio and television, whereas newspapers were of equal importance to US voters. More recent studies have found that globally there is a trend towards television, as the perception is that that medium is the most objective, credible and unbiased (Kraus and Davis, 1978), though studies in nations where newspapers are seen in a similar positive light also find greater reliance upon print media (Siegel, 1983). More recent studies by the Pew Research Center find more Americans are using the Internet to find political information; however, the main sources of information are domestic and global new sites. Interestingly, Americans often use the BBC for a more objective view on US politics; equally those desiring alternative views of events in the Middle East during the 2003 Iraq War accessed Al-Jazeera via the World Wide Web. Few, however, seek their information from source rather than via the mass media when politics is business as usual; such high interest is often the result of conflicts, such as those in Serbia in 1998 and in Iraq in 2003, or during US presidential elections as evidenced in 2004.

KEY FEATURES

There are many aspects to the mediatisation debate, some in terms of its impact on politics, some in terms of its impact on society and others questioning the extent of media power. Cultural studies theorists posit that media culture and consumer culture, or put another way mediatisation and consumerisation, have become intertwined. The core argument is that public consumerisation drives the media towards a market orientation; however, the move from informing to entertaining enforces new views upon society. This could be expressed as a circular process:

public demand = market orientation = mediatisation.

Thus the needs of core groups of consumers, often those whose opinions are sought by media organisations, lead changes in fashions across society more broadly. The result of this has been a move away from issue-based to personality- or image-based news reporting.

Clearly this has a sharp impact upon politics. Kepplinger (2002) finds that German politicians struggle to gain access to the news; in fact it is non-politicians that dominate the news agenda. Thus, it is argued, politicians need to move out of the world of government and advance themselves as personalities; project an image, an emotional and aesthetic dimension to their characters, and foster perceptions of themselves as men or women of the people. Such ploys, whether natural or forced, were successful for a range of leaders including US President Bill Clinton, UK Prime Minister Tony Blair, Brazilian President Fernando Collor de Mello and Italian Prime Minister Silvio Berlusconi. Clinton and Blair courted the news and became media personalities, de Mello and Berlusconi moved from being media moguls straight into the top political jobs. Others made a transition from show business to politics, notable examples being US actors Clint Eastwood, Ronald Reagan and Arnold Schwarznegger. The increasing frequency with which political media stars are proliferating encourage some to note the mutation of politics into a media-friendly circus. The logic behind this are the changes in society and difficulties faced when communicating to a cynical and disengaged public; however, is this the process of mediatisation and does it have a more profound effect?

The mediatisation of politics can be argued to be part of a broader social trend, the mediatisation of society. That what the public see and hear in the media shapes the way that they view the world and themselves and, subsequently, how they act. It is not new to suggest that popular musicians, screen stars or sports personalities are able to lead fashions and news agendas as well as contribute political ideas to the public sphere: simply consider the role of U2's Bono. However, does the constant exposure to polished performers, or those who appear natural in front of a camera when promoting themselves, a new book, film or CD, or a political platform, make the public expect similar from political communicators? Equally does the reliance on the media by political communicators for access to the public and related reliance on the media by the public for political information, offer nothing but skewed perspectives? The fear is that media bias becomes the only real knowledge owned by the public sphere, that access to anything else is limited and reliant on the efforts of individuals.

political communication

119

More recent studies argue that the concept of mediatisation belongs to the 'television era'. It is suggested that in the 'digital' or 'electronic' age, what are often referred to as new media, television is no longer the only source of political information; therefore the public are more able to create their own individual public spheres. This empowerment allows them to be their own information filters; they select what to access, how and when. The future importance of direct, electronic communication methods is argued famously by Manuel Castells (1996), which suggests that mass communication will disappear in the wake of the rise of virtual communities. This in turn means that political communicators are given the opportunity to bypass the media using electronic communications; however, so can a myriad of other political organisations, including pressure groups, terrorists and individuals, so adding to the levels of political noise directed at audiences. This is the case for the cessation of media dependency that mediatisation suggests.

However, if there is no longer such a thing as media dependency, and direct, electronic communications have become the best means of reaching a mass audience, why are communications experts still focusing on traditional media and news management? There are many reasons to be sceptical of the demise of mediatisation:

- The uneven access to technology means such developments focus on one area of the world, and only on certain groups within those societies.
- Access is not unregulated, at the very least by finances in the democratic world, elsewhere access is extremely limited.
- Content is regulated by a variety of laws enforced by service providers and web-masters.
- Even where access is free and content is unregulated, ability hinders the use of freely accessing and imparting communication.
- The rules and norms that are becoming established within the new media environment are enforced on one another by users; sites must look a certain way, use certain design templates. Equally English appears to be the de facto universal language.
- Sites can often be judged in comparison to offline communication, particularly the sites of individual politicians who use this to offer personal views of issues that can contrast with party policy.
- Politics is a minor attraction among web users, outside election campaigns particularly; therefore it may not be worth the development effort.

Clearly, political communication is becoming more web literate, and direct communication is playing some role in the overall campaign strategy. However, new media have not reached the critical mass required for them to offer unfettered access to the mass voting public. Neither are new media employed by the user for gaining political knowledge, at least not to the extent to warrant switching away from traditional media to reach the masses. Hence it remains the role of the media to perform the majority of communication functions within a society; as a result, much of what is in the public sphere is mediatised, it is shaped by media logic until direct electronic communication comes of age. Even then the medium may well still shape the message.

FURTHER READING

The concept of mediatisation was introduced as a social theory by B. Thompson (1990) *Ideology and Modern Culture*. Cambridge: Polity. Studies of the reliance on the media for political information include S. Kraus and D. Davis (1978) *The Effects of Mass Communication on Political Behaviour*. London, PA: Pennsylvania State University Press; A. Siegel (1983) *Politics and the Media in Canada*. Toronto, McGraw-Hill; D. Grondin and C. Grondin (1996) 'Information-seeking activities of party activists', in D.L. Paletz, *Political Communication in Action*. Cresskill, NJ: Hampton Press). 259–76. On the effects of mediatisation of politics and political discourse see G. Mazzolini and W. Shulz '"Mediatization" of politics: A challenge for democracy?', *Political Communication*, 16: 247–61; H.M. Kepplinger (2002) 'Mediatization of politics: Theory and data', *Journal of Communication*, December: 972–86. For a debate on mediatisation, and the role of the internet see W. Shulz (2004) 'Reconstructing mediatization as an analytical concept', *European Journal of Communication*, 19 (1): 87–101; see also Manuel Castells (1996) *The Rise of the Network Society*. London: Blackwell.

political communication

Message/ Messages

> *The message is a short, easily understood piece of communication, often no more than a few words, that conveys information from and about a party, candidate or organisation. Messages in a political context are largely persuasive, so mirroring the majority of the marketing and promotional communication which pervades modern consumerist society.*

ORIGINS AND LINKS

Messages have been used to good effect throughout history. The Bible, Shakespeare's plays, the early use of printed news have all proven to be powerful and are all testament to the use of messages to convey information and to persuade the receiver to act in a certain way or to believe certain things. However research into the power of messages has a much shorter history. Aristotle certainly laid the ground work when arguing that communication had three components: a communicative ideology, an emotional quality and a core argument; but it was not until the 1960s that scholars identified these as being the parts of a message. Therefore a message says something about the communicator and appeals to the emotions and attitudes of the intended receivers in order that the core of the message will be adopted. One can liken messages to branches that grow out of the theme of a campaign. The theme should inform the audience about one particular aspect of the organisation's policy, the message or messages will develop from that theme, or aspects of the theme, memorable phrases, images and arguments.

While the central theme will act as a controlling force on all messages, messages themselves may often contain sub-messages; some taking one aspect of the core message, others altered for a slightly different voter segment. For example, the message on health policy may be to increase spending in order that service is improved. Sub-messages would focus on the 'nuts and bolts' of policy: numbers of staff, improved facilities, rationalisation of service provision, etc. Further messages will focus on the costing of the improvements to service provision, and the potential impact on other policy areas such as tax levels. These messages may then be translated down to local policy level, so talking to key audience members whose concerns reside in a particular area and discussing their unique health care issues. Thus from the trunk of the theme we see a number of branches emerging, each of which would be policy areas, and from those branches, twigs grow out to reach key audience segments with specially targeted messages.

Within modem society, messages are everywhere. They are transmitted by corporate and political organisations in an attempt to alter the behaviour of receivers. Perhaps the most common messages, and the most successful in meeting their objectives, are advertising straplines. When one says 'I'm loving it' it is probably little surprise that McDonalds comes to mind. Advertisements are repeated constantly, and so the images and messages enter our subconsciousness. In a political context this is very important, how else could George W. Bush have branded John Kerry, his opponent in the 2004 US Presidential Election, as a flip-flop – a candidate that constantly changed his mind; equally in the 2005 UK General Election, attempts were made to link the word liar with the image of Tony Blair. McDonalds and Bush were successful, yet while the 'Liar' campaign was memorable among Blair's opponents it appeared to have had little effect on the election result.

Messages are of central importance to any form of political communication, they can be positive or negative, depending on what is perceived to be the most successful strategy and their increasing use and sophistication goes to the heart of debates surrounding the **packaging** of politics and related discussion of an emergent **soundbite culture**.

THE KEY FEATURES

Messages act as heuristic shortcuts, they fill the information gap that exists among the majority of the audience who are unlikely to read party or organisation manifestoes or mission statements, will not access their websites and will recall little or nothing concerning those issues received via traditional news channels. Messages are integrated into news reportage, advertising, public relations material and all communication between the organisation and public for the duration of a campaign. Messages are argued to be of greater importance in the current age of a fragmented electorate and a plethora of media channels (Neumann,

2001). They are able, like many advertising and marketing slogans, to enter our consciousness without really being noticed. This is known as low attention processing (see **media effects**), whereby as we hear these messages repeated over various communication channels, they are slowly remembered and linked to the communicator until we find the messenger and message, and sometimes the person or organisation described in the message, intrinsically linked in our psyche. This is recognised as a phenomenon and is played to in political communication strategies through a process of repeat-remind.

The communication of messages has become more and more sophisticated, in line with developments in commercial advertising. While messages are conveyed in many different ways, they also use a vast array of imagery and devices to capture public attention. In the lead up to the 2005 G8 summit, the meeting of the leaders of the world's eight richest nations, many organisations mobilised to campaign for an increased environmentalist focus or for greater aid for the poorest nations. The Live 8 event was a powerful way of communicating a message, 'Make Poverty History', and used the performances of a range of pop and comedy performers to appeal to a wide audience. In contrast, environmental pressure group Greenpeace employed a web-based video 'Mr & Mrs Smith' to deliver the message 'Don't let Blair be Mr Bush's puppet: act on climate change now!' The film showed a Blair puppet, dressed symbolically as a female prostitute, performing an oral sex act upon an anonymous but large and overtly affluent American male until the 'puppet' was covered in crude oil. The communication style was clearly aimed at an apolitical, young, UK audience; there was no similar film directed at any other G8 member's public, suggesting the power of Blair over Bush and the importance of action based in the UK.

Why would such a message work? There are various ways of understanding the components of messages and how they are able to persuade receivers to take heed and recall as well as act upon the message (see O'Keefe (2002), chapter 9, or any persuasion text book); however this particular case employs certain features that encourage recall. To some the image of Blair will be humorous as well as intriguing, so encouraging attention. As the narrative ensues the imagery is fairly shocking, with the relevance questionable maintaining the audiences' fascination; the closing scene is the 'aha' moment which links into the voiceover delivering the core message. In the modern society, where we find ourselves faced with increasing amounts of persuasive communication, such techniques are of ultra-importance for getting the message across.

THE ACADEMIC AND PRACTICAL DEBATES

There is no doubt of the pervasive nature of messages in our society, many of which have political motivations. A major question is, however, do messages have any effect? Many studies argue that the public suffer from information, or message, overload, therefore are unable to retain much information. While many may associate McDonalds with 'I'm loving it', does anyone when they subsequently hear or read the phrase automatically fancy a Big Mac? Even if it is the case with this example, does the cynicism about politicians and lack of belief in politicians generally prevent political messages permeating our subconscious? Actually many argue that this is not the case. Because we pay little real attention to political news and the messages contained in the news or in advertisements then the messages are used as the fundamental basis of our knowledge. US voters accepted that John Kerry was a flip-flop, they did not investigate whether this was a fact, instead the phrase appeared to permeate **popular culture**, and was the number one characteristic that voters linked to Kerry during opinion polling. Thus it seems his credibility became irrevocably damaged through the employment of the message and its acceptance by the audience. This is an example of the power of a message; however consider how many messages fail!

Persuasion theory suggests that the amount of information and the public's general lack of interest will lead to greater influence being awarded to the peripheral aspects of communication. Therefore a message will be retained if it is simple to remember, but more importantly if it is believable in some way. The believability, or level of acceptance, depends on the credibility of the source and whether the receiver likes the source for some reason, and the credibility of the message itself and whether the receiver chooses firstly to take heed and subsequently to accept it. These factors, along with the techniques discussed above, highlight the importance of design. Yet there is one further factor: that is, receipt.

Designers of messages are unable to control the way in which they are received. They can control the medium they use, be it print, television or the Internet, and whether the communication is direct or indirect – mediated or not – but messages are also decoded by each audience member according to their individual thought processes. If we consider the Greenpeace film, some audience members will find it offensive while others will view it as humorous and satirical. Equally some audience members will agree that Blair has power over Bush, others may not. The differences in decoding, just on these two aspects, have important ramifications. The negativity will turn off some audience members, possibly leading them to view Greenpeace in a negative light, especially if they are offended by the 'oral sex' that is suggested in the film. Others may find it amusing yet view the film cynically, believing that it is a cheap shot at gaining attention; again Greenpeace could suffer from the negative decoding by the audience. Equally, if Blair's influence over Bush is doubted it will fail to mobilise viewers to lobby Blair, thus not meeting its core objective. Debates on decoding often argue that this human ability acts as a natural safeguard against the ability of organisations to persuade the public; in contrast however, some argue that the message still filters through despite audience members' attempts to reject them; particularly if they enter the audience's subconscious via the low attention processing route. While studies have shown both processes at work, all we do know is that some messages are accepted by the public sphere at large and some are consigned to the waste basket of communication history; it remains difficult to predict the fate of any one message.

FURTHER READING

Messages are discussed at length in most books covering persuasive communication; two good examples are D. O'Keefe (2002) *Persuasion: Theory & Research*, 2nd edn, Thousand Oaks: Sage, chapter 9; R.M. Perloff (2003) *The Dynamics of Persuasion*, 2nd edn, Manwah, NJ: Lawrence Erlbaum, chapter 7. For an interesting discussion on the way in which messages are received see A. Lang (2002) 'The limited capacity model of mediated message processing', *Journal of Communication*, Winter 2000, pp. 46–70. On processing messages and in particular the differences between high level and low level processing see R.E. Petty, J.T. Capiocco and D. Schumann (1983) 'Central and peripheral routes to advertising effectiveness: the moderating role of involvement,' *Journal of Consumer Research*, 10 (2): 135–46; this article details the very useful elaboration likelihood model.

Negativity

Negativity is a tool of communication that stresses the weaknesses in opponents' arguments, behaviour, personality or credentials for government. It is linked to making attacks on electoral opponents, thus undermining the candidate or party, suggesting that the sponsor of the attack could do better.

ORIGINS AND LINKS

The fact that negativity is studied mainly as a feature in **political advertising** means that its origins as an area of academic study lie in the nation where advertising is most used by political parties: the USA. The funding of political parties in most other parts of the world means that advertising is largely less sophisticated and attacks have to be made using different media. This does not mean, however, that negativity in political campaigning began with the heavy spending campaign of successful US presidential candidate Dwight Eisenhower in 1956; most candidates in election contests have been drawn to make negative references to their opponents. British Prime Minister Benjamin Disraeli described his Liberal opponent William Gladstone as 'an unprincipled maniac ... an extraordinary mixture of envy, vindictiveness, hypocrisy and superstition' and perhaps worst of all for Victorian English society 'never a gentleman'. In contrast to the personal attack, attacks on the arms of state have been a useful tool of any would-be radical or revolutionary. Russian revolutionary leader Lenin and democratically elected Russian Prime Minister Boris Yeltsin, acting almost a hundred years apart, both attacked the failures of, in the first case, tsarism and, in the second, communism. Hitler attacked the weakness of the Weimar government in Germany, while Castro led a propaganda war against the Cuban Batista government. However, the systematic use of negativity in a democratic context is something new and is pioneered in the American model of campaigning.

The increased, and wider, use of negativity is seen as a feature of **Americanisation**, as political parties look to the US as the model for a more professionalised campaign. It is also linked to the increased use of political **marketing**; however, this is somewhat confusing as few corporations would consider using negativity in a campaign. Thus it is the effects on the public that command most attention. While debates question negativity's effectiveness, they also raise questions about its contribution to **cynicism**, the breakdown in trust between the public and politicians and the disengagement of the public from electoral activity.

KEY FEATURES

The key feature is that the central theme of the particular aspect of the campaign, be it a series of advertisements, one single advertisement, or an entire campaign, focuses on attacking the opponent rather than putting forward an argument that details the positive reasons for why the sponsor should be elected. An example of this type of advertisement is shown in Figure 9. A television advertisement, it was sponsored by Democrat Jim Hodges as part of his campaign to remain as Governor of South Carolina in 2002.

This advertisement focuses entirely on Mark Sanford, there is no mention of Hodges, his opponent, except at the very start of the advertisement where the sponsor, by US law, must be named. However, studies of recall suggest it is the images and linked voice-overs, when repeated, that have the impact. The inclusion of the picture of Sanford stamped with 'WRONG FOR SOUTH CAROLINA' but including his web address, almost gives the appearance of it being an official statement by Sanford himself.

Elsewhere, negative messages are less sophisticated. A famous example from the 2001 UK general election that enjoyed much attention is shown in Figure 10. This is far more amusing, though remains clearly negative and says little about why the sponsor, the Labour Party and Prime Minister Tony Blair, would be a better leader than Conservative leader William Hague. It just presents an amalgamation of Hague and former Prime Minister Margaret Thatcher suggesting, one assumes, a return to Thatcherism.

THE ACADEMIC AND PRACTICAL DEBATES

Whether we think negativity is appropriate in democratic politics, particularly in advertising, or not, we are more likely to remember it than the traditional 'talking head' television spot of a party leader extolling his or her virtues and those of the party. In fact, the more it fits into what we would expect from mainstream, non-political communication the better

key concepts

Video	Audio
	In Congress, Mark Sanford tried to privatise Social Security, giving our retirement to Wall Street.
	Sanford's plan would leave senior [citizens] without protection from companies like Enron and Worldcom.
	That's why Wall Street bankers are backing Sanford.
	Mark Sanford: wrong on Social Security: wrong for South Carolina.

This text is adapted from http://medialit.med.sc.edu/HarvardLessonplan.htm

Figure 9   *A negative television advertisement (Courtesy of Frank Baker)*

Negativity

Get out and vote.
Or they get in.

Figure 10   *Negative poster from the UK 2001 general election (from BBC News website. For the report and a further example see: http://news.bbc.co.uk/vote2001/hi/english/features/ newsid_1359000/1359332.stm)*

it seems. If only because it is less likely to be switched off by the viewer. Therefore making the message eye-catching is important. However, if the message is negative how is it received?

Research with US audiences show a high level of recall, particularly among the lower-educated, lower-income groups; the negative messages are also more likely to be believed by those groups. However, the fact that the sponsor's name is attached means that a negative perception is also earned by that sponsor. Ansolabehere and Iyengar (1995) found that it is seen as part of a 'dirty tricks' war and so negativity appeals only to loyal supporters of the sponsor, and is more likely to disengage floating voters from the democratic process than win them over to one side or another. Elsewhere there is less negativity, and it remains a novelty. However, research in the UK found that negativity is significantly unpopular and its use in the Labour Party's campaign in 2001 was one contributory factor towards the low turnout at that general election.

Nevertheless, politicians do not seem to be learning from this. The 2004 US presidential election saw, in the words of *Washington Post* journalists, 'an unprecedented level of negativity with each side attacking the other to a far greater extent than they have offered pledges to the US public should they be elected'. Incumbent candidate, George W. Bush, appeared the most negative, constantly labelling challenger John Kerry as 'undecided' or a 'flip-flop' on the key issues, such as the War on Terrorism. The effect was a Bush victory, though it is impossible to assess the impact of the negative campaigning at this time. This is in contrast to the effects of a negative campaign in the French presidential election of 2002. The main challengers, Prime Minster Lionel Jospin and incumbent Jacques Chirac, fought each other mercilessly, resulting in Jospin's vote being split across a wide range of left-wing supporters and leaving space for neo-fascist extremist Jean-Marie Le Pen to receive sufficient votes to be in the second round of voting against Chirac. *Le Monde* argued that the negativity confused the voters, causing many to vote for alternatives as both 'seemed as bad as one another'. The US 2004 election result may be an indication that Bush's negative campaigning had resonance with the voters in a way that Chiracs and Jospin's did not.

FURTHER READING

The effect of negativity, as an area of academic study, is in relative infancy. The most thorough study has been on the use of negativity in US political advertising, for which see S. Ansolabehere and S. Iyengar (1995) *Going Negative*. New York: Free Press; though their conclusions are debated in C.J. Dolan (2004) 'Two cheers for negative ads', in D. Shultz (ed.), *Lights, Camera, Campaign: Media, Politics and Political Advertising*. New York: Peter Lang. For a useful recent study in the UK see J. Dermody and R. Scullion (2002) 'Perceptions of negative political advertising. Meaningful or menacing?', *International Journal of Advertising*, 19 (2): 201–23. The media are always useful commentators on the conduct of elections; therefore for recent election analysis refer to key domestic newspapers.

News Management

News management is the strategic communication of messages, via the media, in order to further political goals. It is concerned with the control of information, and the way in which political information is reported, by political organisations.

ORIGINS AND LINKS

Traditionally, news management was solely about the creation and dissemination of press releases from the political organisations to the media; an activity which took place in an environment of mutual reliance. While it is still the case that political organisations need the media in order to communicate to the public, it is not always the case that this is reciprocated. **News values** have altered dramatically over the last 20 years, with public service broadcasting and news coverage being reduced in favour of public entertainment. Hence it is now more difficult for the political organisation to gain coverage. This has led many organisations, political parties in particular, to employ specialists to engage in news management. Their role is to make political communication more attractive to news gatherers, as well as to add **spin** which is designed to prevent the eventual story being framed in a way that is in opposition to the communication strategy. Studies in the UK have argued that this process is becoming highly professionalised, in terms of both practice and personnel. They also highlight that, since 1997, the concept and practice of news management has moved to the centre of the political process (Jones, 1996; Davis, 2002). This leads to a discussion of a public relations democracy or the **public relations state**; news management being a central tool of the public relations officer.

KEY FEATURES

The central feature of a news management strategy is to control the media news agenda in order to influence public opinion. While this presupposes a direct link between the media agenda and public opinion, which is disputed (see media effects), the notion is that if all coverage is as favourable as possible, public opinion will be more supportive of the policy, party, government or organisation. All organisations with an interest in an issue will attempt to gain control of the agenda, some are able to, some are not; journalists and editors are argued to act as the gatekeepers in a pluralist democracy. Therefore we find some groups resorting to drastic, and usually direct, action in an attempt to seize media attention for their cause.

Within a system where news management is standard practice, the media and the political organisations are often viewed as being two sides locked in a battle. Journalists argue that they do not fight political communicators, they simply fight to get at the truth on behalf of the public. Politicians often offer the rebuttal that, without the gatekeepers, agenda-setters and media biases, they would be able to present their case to the public in the way the public would want. It is because of this that some talk of a vicious circle existing, in which media, politics and the public are all unwittingly embroiled. The reason for this is the differing logic each party works to. Political organisations wish to speak to the public; the media however need to be market-oriented and avoid becoming the propaganda tool of any one group. Some politicians seize control of aspects of the media, as Italian President Berlusconi has done since his election in 2000; others work on a system of semi-patronage, such as the relationship between the British government and the BBC or the support offered to the US Republicans by Fox TV; the rest must try and link their communication to the media logic without submitting altogether (see Mazzoleni, 1987).

Governments, however, have major advantages over their rivals in developing effective news management strategies. They have the resources to employ personnel and have a budget to cover the dissemination of information. Furthermore they are constantly making news by dint of the fact that they make policy. Thus, while they are unable to determine the nature of coverage, they are able to ensure the lion's share of column inches and television pictures and time. Studies of news management find there are differing strategies according to the motives and object of the message, as is illustrated in Table 2.

Table 2   *News management strategies*

	Media-centred motive	Political motive
Personality-centred	Image management Visual images Emotionalised mass message	Political attacks or comparisons Negativity
Policy-centred	Pseudo-event Dramatisation/Action shots Informational and targeted Multi-layered	Framing and spin Highlight outcomes Agenda leading

The purpose of a media-centred motive is to gain favourable coverage; this often links into a **permanent campaign** strategy. This can centre on a leader and will be an attempt at positively **branding** the organisation using strong visuals and emotional appeals. Alternatively, policies are introduced within a media-friendly context: a leader's visit for example.

Policy announcements tend to present information but are often targeted at key groups in society through their presentation at different levels or using different media. In contrast, communication with a political motive will usually attack or compare a leader with opponents, employing **negativity** to win control over the agenda. Similar tactics are employed when introducing policy: the communication will be framed already, have spin embedded and be designed to determine the way it is covered. Thus opponents will have to react and as such will be playing catch-up in the battle for the news.

THE ACADEMIC AND PRACTICAL DEBATES

At the heart of the debates on the prioritisation of news management is the discussion of blame. Is it the fault of the media, or the introduction of media consultants into political communication? Mazzoleni and Shultz (1999) argue that political communication has become 'mediatized', designed specifically for the market-orientated media, thus that there is little information designed for public consumption and so the continued good health of democracy. In fact they argue that voters are being transformed, not into critical consumers, but into passive spectators of electoral campaigns, policy debates and decisions that affect nations' futures. The alternative view is that media consultants are the ones driving change. They are bringing to politics techniques and tools that do not necessarily fit with the way in which pluralist democracy is conducted (Mancini, 1999). However, both of these arguments tend to miss the logic at play behind the use of news management strategies; while both politics and the media follow opposing goals both are at fault as well as being trapped.

The effects on the public gain most attention; it is argued almost universally that news management techniques do a disservice to democracy. While some would argue that such practices are necessary, they put a case forward for a reform in the relations between political organisations, particularly governments, and the media. However, few can suggest exactly what shape these 'better' relations will take. While some nations do not employ the raft of strategies and strategists that are commonplace in the US and UK, many other nations face difficulties due to the conflict between media and politics. While it is a feature of the UK and US that the '**spin-doctor**' becomes as famous as the politicians, James Carville and Alistair Campbell being excellent examples, studies of political communication in Germany, Spain and Denmark all note the increased use of professionals that manage media relations. Thus, although

key concepts

news management is seen as having negative effects on politics, few seem willing or able to end the vicious cycle that centres on the fight for the news agenda and public opinion.

FURTHER READING

A good introduction to media–politics relations can be found in G. Mazzoleni (1987) 'Media logic and party logic in campaign coverage: The Italian general election of 1983', *European Journal of Communication*, 2 (1): 81–103. There are also regular references in a comparative perspective throughout the contributions to D.L. Swanson and P. Mancini (1996) *Politics, Media and Modern Democracy: An International Study of Innovations in Electoral Campaigning and their Consequences*. London: Praeger. For a case study of the UK see N. Jones (1996) *Soundbites and Spin Doctors*. London: Cassell; A. Davis (2002) *Public Relations Democracy: Public Relations, Politics and the Mass Media in Britain*. Manchester: Manchester University Press. For a critique of the press 'intrusion' into politics see G. Mazzoleni and W. Schulz (1999) "Mediatization" of politics: A challenge for democracy', *Political Communication*, 16: 247–61; the role of consultants is critiqued in P. Mancini (1999) 'New frontiers in political professionalism', *Political Communication*, 16: 231–45; a more even-handed discussion is offered by K. Sanders, T. Bale and M.J. Canel (1999) 'Managing sleaze: Prime ministers and news management in Conservative Britain and Socialist Spain', *European Journal of Communication*, 14 (4): 461–86.

News Values

News Values describe the currency that journalists and news editors attach to a particular story, type of story or even an individual. The concept is that some things are more newsworthy because they attract an audience, while others quite simply do not.

A 1996 study by Dearing and Rogers, of the role of the media in determining the campaign agenda highlighted the increasing power of the media. While there have always been stories that gain coverage, as is highlighted in Kevin Williams's history of mass communication in Britain the title of which, *Get Me A Murder A Day*, is borrowed from the motto of the founder of the *Daily Mail* and is indicative of the attitude of many working in news production, that scandal, sleaze and gore are what the people want. Of course this is a simplification of news values; however, the increased merger of information and entertainment, what some call **infotainment**, is argued to have had an effect on the way politics is reported.

A number of studies have shown the reduction of column inches or programming minutes awarded to parliaments in the UK, France and Germany (see Negrine, 1998). It is argued that the media have abandoned their 'sacerdotal' stance, which means that parliaments and parties were treated deferentially and awarded news coverage because of their importance within society. Studies of the media suggest they now adopt a far more pragmatic view. All news items are judged against one another; editors decide which stories will be seen as important by their audience, will satisfy audience demands and will attract a larger audience. Blumler and Gurevitch (1995: 56) argue that there is a mental map, a news value scale, with sacerdotal at one end and pragmatic at the other. Automatic media coverage is awarded to those organisations that are placed at the sacerdotal end. Arguably, political institutions are placed closer to the pragmatic end of the scale, replaced by the majority of popular newspapers with celebrities and sports stars.

Clearly, news values are not simply about gaining or not gaining coverage. News values possessed within the editorial team will also dominate the framing of a political news story, what they feel should be at the top of the agenda as well as which actors feature and which are sidelined. While politicians **mediatise** their communication and use **news management** strategies to capture the **agenda**, the media hold the ultimate power in deciding what is news and how it should be reported (Fuller, 1997).

KEY FEATURES

Access to the news programming awarded to political organisations depends on five factors as identified in Blumler and Gurevitch (1995: 95).

key concepts

1 The ideological leanings of the media organisation.
2 The status, or importance, of the politician.
3 The extent to which news should be balanced politically.
4 The space available.
5 Decisions on the appropriateness of the story.

These clearly give significant power to the media. While at least three can be linked to the political bias of the media organisation, as it may well believe an individual is of lesser status and so deem the story inappropriate if it does not agree with their politics. Other news organisations take a position on the other extreme; they demand that all news coverage should be balanced, in other words no group can be given air time unless their opponents also take part. This can be invoked during election campaigns to give the image of objectivity and is found to frustrate groups trying to communicate to the public using the cheapest most available means.

It is argued, thus, that political organisations are forced to mediatise their communication in order to fit with the media news values and gain coverage. Is there a blueprint for such activity, or is it as much a pragmatic process on behalf of the political communicators as it is in the news room? The fact is, the audience is in charge, news values are determined by the market orientation of the majority of mass media organisations; therefore it is the societal news values that appear important. When looking at the line of reasoning in favour of the emotionalisation and aestheticisation of political communication, and of politics itself, the increased promotion of style and image and the need to legitimise the political system; all arguments link to the requirements of the voting publics.

Thus news values are central to determining both the campaign strategy and the agenda that exists within the public sphere. So what are the key features of the modern news agenda?

1 Personalisation. It appears that the personality, or emotional and human side, of political actors is important. Sometimes policies are attributed to single actors, as was the case during German Chancellor Schroeder's 2002 campaign. Alternatively the private life of the political actor becomes paramount, or attention is focused on their personal characteristics, as the Austrian media highlighted during Jorge Haider's campaign which led him to accentuate personal over political.
2 Mistakes. Clearly the media enjoy highlighting transgressions throughout their news coverage. While these may not always fit into

the categories of scandal and sleaze, contradictions in campaign messages, divisions within parties or coalitions or mistakes of individual politicians are standard fare.

3   Wedge issues. The media seem to dislike issues where there is a lack of clear space between parties. They prefer issues where there are clear divisions and on which they can take a stand.

4   Partisanship. There are arguments that the audience do not want pure objectivity, rather that they want the media to express their biases. Thus newspapers tend to cater for one segment of the voting public. Television news and political magazine programmes can also be found to express bias, often framed as presenting the questions the 'man in the street' would ask.

5   Editorialising. Donsbach (1997) found that the majority of coverage of the 1994 German Bundestag election featured commentary but little information. This is part of a trend where the journalists make sense of political stories for its audience. Clearly this can bias reporting, even when this is unintentional, and offer a skewed perspective of politics.

Political communication adheres to these news values by promoting the personal, the rest is largely outside their influence and a side-effect of a campaign that cannot be controlled.

THE ACADEMIC AND PRACTICAL DEBATES

Recent data suggest that around 70–80 per cent of the public gain their political information from watching television news. Therefore if the supply of news is limited, or political news is derogated to marginal timeslots, the public do not receive the information they require. This criticism lies at the heart of the dumbing down debate and is laid at the door of the media and the politician alike. The problem is that the debate makes no sense when we look at the reasoning behind the scaling of news values and political actors' changes of style.

It is argued that the public require their political information to be framed in emotionality and desire to see more personal and less political information. They also require politics to have aesthetic qualities. Equally, they seem largely unwilling to sit and watch serious news but prefer it to be packaged as infotainment. Therefore a strategic approach to determining news values seems to be common sense. The media logic is to gain an audience, largely due to needing advertising and sponsorship revenue. In turn, the political logic is to get the message across to the public. If there are only certain types of information that the public will take in, then it clearly makes sense to package information in a way that reaches the audience. Perhaps more research is required into media and political communication effects; currently, however, we appear to have a debate in which practitioners and academics are talking past one another, each blind to the logic of the other's argument.

FURTHER READING

A very useful introduction is offered in S. Fuller (1997) *News Values: Ideas for an Information Age*. Chicago: University of Chicago Press. On the reduction of coverage and importance of media news values see J. Blumler and M. Gurevitch (1995) *The Crisis of Public Communication*. London: Routledge; R. Negrine (1998) *Parliament and the Media: A Study of Britain, Germany and France*. London: Pinter. For a case study of news values during an election see W. Donsbach (1997) 'Media thrust in the German Bundestag election, 1994: News values and professional norms in political communication', *Political Communication*, 14: 149–70. See also J.W. Dearing and M. Rogers (1996) *Agenda-Setting*. London: Sage.

Packaging

Packaging refers to the way in which politics is presented to the public in democratic societies, either directly or through the mass media. It is increasingly argued that electorally competitive political parties, politicians, governments and their policies are sold in the same way as fast-moving consumer goods, and therefore politicians adopt and adapt a range of selling techniques from the commercial sector. The packaging of political communication, into short phrases and easily remembered images, is argued to hinder in-depth public understanding of politics. Commentators suggest it enhances and exaggerates peripheral aspects in an attempt to win over the voter, but fails to engage with the real societal issues or debates.

139

ORIGINS AND LINKS

The term 'packaging' was first applied by Franklin (1994) to describe the way in which politics in the UK is presented, though the practice of attaching gloss to communication has a long tradition. Since the late 1980s, as part of the general debate surrounding the **Americanisation** and **professionalisation** of political communication, it has been recognised that politicians increasingly concentrate on the presentation of their policies, both in opposition and in government. In rebutting the arguments of those who argue this to be unnecessary, Lord Young, Minister for Trade and Industry in 1988, declared 'the government's policies are like cornflakes; if they are not marketed they will not sell'. This admission represented an important change in political communication; while we expect parties to use sales techniques during the **election campaign**, governments now also see a need to engage in a permanent process of salesmanship, presenting each policy using language and imagery that appeals to the electorate. These developments link to the idea of the **public relations state**, the practice of **permanent campaigning** and **political marketing**. Academic studies therefore focus on the way in which all public representations of the party or government are being managed and controlled. Political statements are written for the media, include **soundbites**, and are designed to be media-friendly; equally party leaders may be chosen on the basis that they are photogenic and present the right **image**.

THE KEY FEATURES

Some academics and journalists argue that the selection of party leaders such as the UK's Tony Blair, former US President Bill Clinton or Labour's Helen Clark in New Zealand was due to their ability to manage their media image. These leaders' ability to perform, in a variety of contexts, allowed them to build up a media personality that arguably contributed to their electoral success. The recognition of the importance of the leader in creating a political 'product' has led many parties to consider who to select as leader. Alternatively, parties or campaigns are formed around high-profile performers: Austria's Jorge Haider or the late flamboyant Dutch politician Pym Fortyun, and to some extent the role of former Labour MP and latter-day television show host Robert Kilroy-Silk in the success of the UK Independence Party at the UK 2004 European Parliament elections. These are instances when the package is personalised.

Policy initiatives are also packaged. In both the UK and the USA the war against Iraq in 2003 was packaged as necessary due to the potential of Saddam Hussein to develop a nuclear weapons capability. In fact, such packaging is everyday practice in every democracy, the benefits of a policy will be advertised at every opportunity in order to convince the voter that this is the correct course of action. Governments will also release figures, accompanied where possible by upbeat televisual pictures, for unemployment, greenhouse gas emissions, terrorists arrested, all manner of events, to package themselves as successful. What is more worrying is when figures that indicate failures are buried beneath a bigger news story. The practice of packaging is therefore omnipresent, a central feature of political communication. Arguably most of the audience are unaware of the packaging process – so differing from commercial advertising and packaging – thus concerns are raised about this practice.

THE ACADEMIC AND PRACTICAL DEBATES

The main reason for politics to be packaged is twofold: first, due to shifts in media reporting of politics; secondly, due to the increasing cynicism of, and difficulty in reaching, the consumerist voter. Clearly these two factors are linked. Within the majority of democracies politicians have to rely on the media for the large majority of communication between themselves and the electorate. Few political parties are able to engage in sustained direct communication with the voters, all communication is therefore mediated by the newspapers and television news channels. In an attempt to receive publicity from an increasingly ratings-driven media, all competing for the same audiences, politicians must make their communication media-friendly. They have to provide a real story, make their announcements interesting and attractive, offer exclusives, and their spokespersons must perform well on camera or in print. Political leaders also try and communicate their message through an alternative format, they will appear on television chat shows so presenting their image in a different way, creating awareness of themselves and their party and hopefully raising interest in their other, more serious, political activity.

The purpose behind this is to reach the voter, because it is often argued that the voter is cynical of political messages and will avoid political news. While the public is not disinterested in politics, they appear disinterested in politicians, mistrustful of their promises and claims, and so the parties find it difficult to find a mode of communication that is sufficiently convincing to win over voters with weak or no party loyalties. The packaging therefore takes many forms. It involves altering the format

of party broadcasts, using language and imagery that borrows from **popular culture**, targeting a range of different media outlets and seeking to project personality and character in order to engender trust and credibility. Governments also use public service broadcasting and public information not only to inform the public of such things as voting in the Scottish Parliament and Welsh Assembly, the announcements of the date for referenda on joining the European Union or initiatives such as the Citizen's Charter, but also to promote the political views of the party in government.

While the latter practice of politicising public information is universally criticised because these broadcasts are traditionally objective and should not be biased, not all of this packaging is seen as negative. John Street (2004) argues that as politicians use other media to promote themselves, particularly appearing on chat shows and other popular culture television formats, they are providing the public with an alternative and more human view of the political world. This can break down the perspective that politicians are detached and out of touch and allow voters to judge them on their human merits; what sort of man or woman they are, what background they have and how they represent the person in the street. This then forms a perception in the minds of the public that combines the practical or political issues with the more personal and emotional appeals of the party and its representatives. Critics, however, argue this is central to the trend towards the **dumbing down** of politics. Packaging, they argue, promotes style over substance, image over policy. Thus voters may choose a president, for example Clinton because he is willing to play saxophone on prime-time television, but have little real idea of how well he will manage the economy or his stance on welfare spending. This argument gives the electorate little credit; however, there are also real fears for the future of political communication.

These fears relate to the fact that all that may separate the parties is their ability to package themselves. That as the culture of political communication changes, then the public will increasingly judge parties and governments on the way in which they communicate. Real political debate will be marginalised as politicians fight for the hearts of voters through their appearances on chat shows, the representations of themselves as caring family-oriented people and the way in which they demonstrate that they relate to ordinary people. Blame is also posited with the media who, it is argued, are inclined to emphasise dissent within parties or focus on the peripheral or amusing and not on the important issues. While this may not fully describe the current situation, there are fears that as parties compete for media space, and the media compete for audiences, politics will be marginalised in favour of entertainment; thus politics will have to become entertainment and politicians entertainers to receive coverage. However, some would argue that the latter is necessary to reach the public anyway. Stephen Coleman's research on how to attract more viewers to politics discussed opening up the Houses of Parliament in the UK to the style of scrutiny allowed by popular reality television programme *Big Brother* (2003). It seems that such visions are not as unrealistic as it would appear at first glance. Across Europe and North America politics is increasingly becoming personalised and packaged for the media in an attempt to win voters.

FURTHER READING

An early and still very useful study is offered in N. Postman (1987) *Amusing Ourselves to Death: Public Discourse in the Age of Show Business*. London: Methuen. The concept of packaging is critiqued in B. Franklin (2004) *Packaging Politics* (2nd edn). London: Arnold. A justification from a UK perspective is offered in S. Coleman (2003) *A Tale of Two Houses: The House of Commons, the Big Brother House and the People at Home*. London: Hansard Society. A history is provided by M. Scammell (1995) *Designer Politics*. Basingstoke: Macmillan.

Permanent Campaigning

political communication

143

Permanent campaigning refers to the use of office by elected individuals and organisations (governments, parties of government, members of parliament, congress or similar elected houses) to build and maintain popular support.

The term 'permanent campaigning' was coined by Pat Cadell, an advisor to newly elected US President Jimmy Carter in 1976. Cadell's memo advised Carter that campaigning could no longer cease with election victory but that there was a need to court the American voter throughout a presidency. Journalist Sidney Blumenthal recognised similar practices intensifying, initially during the Reagan presidency and then throughout the Clinton years. Hence, communications are now seen as almost as much a role of government as fiscal policy, and the permanent campaign is embedded as a feature of modern government.

The reasons for the development of permanent campaigning largely rest with the nature of the modern, or postmodern, electorate. Election campaigns are no longer purely designed to mobilise a party or candidate's supporters; dealignment means that it is the floating voter that is the most valuable commodity to electoral hopefuls. However, these voters are not simply convinced by short-term campaigning techniques, or at least large sections are not. Economic and rational choice models of voting argue that voters take several factors into consideration when making their choice within the voting booth. Important factors are past record, a largely perception-based image within which we include credibility and competence, and their perception of who appears best to manage the nation in the future. Hence the long term has become prioritised among voters, and so parties in government need to sustain the support of the electorate over each policy decision. Hence, in 1997, UK Prime Minister Tony Blair instructed his newly elected MPs: 'Today is day one of the campaign to win a second term – don't let one of you forget that.' On a similar theme, former presidential candidate Barry Goldwater argued 'every communication does something to the brand image – if you can control it, then it must all be positive'. Such statements reinforce Blumenthal's opinion, campaigning has become the new ideology underpinning government (1980).

KEY FEATURES

There are a number of features of campaigning that it is argued have infested the modern practice of governing. It is useful to identify these and relate them to a term of office, as opposed to the period of a campaign when normal politics is marginalized.

- Campaigning is short term: thus governing will be peppered with campaigns on numerous policies. In the UK the decision to go to war

key concepts

against Saddam Hussein's Iraq was a protracted and unprecedentedly professional campaign designed to change public opinion.

- Campaigning is necessarily adversarial: therefore differences between political parties should be clearer on the major issues. While the Iraq War brought parties in the US, UK and across Europe closer together, divisions remain on domestic policies as parties continually attempt to win public support for their line. On immigration issues, French neo-fascist Le Pen's Front Nationale often try to steal support from president and fellow right-winger Jacques Chirac, a feature that the French media often see as damaging.

- Campaigning is persuasive: hence governments will employ greater levels of propagandist rhetoric and we will see greater use of communication experts and public relations officers, often termed spin-doctors, to manage communication. Recent studies find that the use of consultants is prevalent across Europe and the Americas and that their chief task is to manage communication between and during elections.

Therefore we find terms of government to consist of a series of campaigns, each pitting party against party, or in some systems president versus prime minister or one house of government, in a battle for public support. As a result, public opinion, if tracked reasonably frequently and when the parties are close to each other in terms of support, can be constantly shifting from government to opposition and back.

However, Ormstein and Mann (2000) note that there are also a range of political and societal features that underpin the introduction of permanent campaigning. These are:

- the weakening of party organizations and resulting centralization of communication away from the local level;
- the rise of non-electoral or interest group politics competing, and often winning, public attention;
- technological advancements in communications facilitating 24/7 news gathering;
- improvements in polling and public opinion gathering allow greater links to be made between cause and effect (what caused a drop in support, what can provide an increase);
- the need for campaign funding, something that is a vast industry in the USA but is faced by most parties where there is no state funding policy;
- the higher stakes; or greater likelihood of losing support and so falling from power, for a government that is active. The premise here is that

the more that is done, the more that can be criticized by opponents and so the greater potential for public support to be lost.

Thus these features all interrelate with one another to create an impetus for permanent campaigning. Some argue it is necessary and unavoidable, others posit that it damages governing credibility as the focus shifts from political management to political communication.

KEY DEBATES

Studies into permanent campaigning largely stem from the US, where the practice has been embedded for decades and so the effects are becoming visible. Ormstein and Mann (2000) argue that public participation has been weakened and disengagement and cynicism rife. This may seem contradictory; that parties that focus more on public opinion, and a permanent marketing strategy, should appear more out of touch. However, it is the constant persuasive communication, in a tit-for-tat battle with opponents, which leaves audiences confused and cynical. They believe both sides are selling themselves, just like soap powder brands arguing their product is best, and thus they ignore both. Such trends are exacerbated in the USA by the use of highly negative, and often misleading, attack advertisements which can lead to high-profile battles via the television. Voters find this a less than edifying spectacle and reject the message and the messenger.

But is there an alternative? Critics argue for a more consensual style of government. Opponents in the US, France and the UK should not criticise one another for the sake of doing so, but should take a more constructive role in policy development. This is more common in systems where there are coalition governments, but coalition groups may still campaign against outsiders to that group. However, agreements between Democrats and Republicans in the US, and the UK Labour government and Conservative opposition, led to criticisms of Democrats and Conservatives as being ineffective in representing public opinion. Vaughan (2003) argues that the permanent campaign is a necessary tool by which the office of the US President 'survives and thrives', and in a similar vein former UK journalist, politician and campaign strategist Peter Mandelson argued in a conference presentation that 'ongoing communication was central to the legitimacy of the political system'. This leaves us with a perhaps unanswerable question: does politics need more or better permanent campaigning, or less? Academics and practitioners appear divided on this; therefore perhaps only time will tell.

An early US insider study can be found in S. Blumenthal (1980) *The Permanent Campaign: Inside the World of Elite Political Operatives.* Boston, MA: Beacon. For a more in-depth review of the nature and effects see N.J. Ormstein and T.E. Mann (2000) *The Permanent Campaign and Its Future.* Washington, DC: American Enterprise Institute and The Brookings Institute. For UK studies see D. Nimmo (2000) 'The permanent campaign: Marketing as a governing tool', in B.I. Newman, *Handbook of Political Marketing,.* London: Sage; N. Sparrow and J. Turner (2001) 'The permanent campaign – The integration of market research techniques in developing strategies in a more uncertain political climate', *European Journal of Marketing,* 35 (9–10): 984–1002. A recent, highly useful study, is J.S. Vaughan (2003) 'Presidents and the permanent campaign: towards a new theory of presidential elections', paper presented to the Annual National Conference of the Midwest Political Science Association, at http://mpsa.indiana.edu/conf2003papers/1032042496.pdf

— Political Advertising —

> *As with all advertising, a political advertisement is a purposely placed piece of communication, using a range of media, designed to garner positive feelings towards the sponsor.*

ORIGINS AND LINKS

Political advertising, in one form or another, has been a feature of campaigning ever since groups began competing over public support. However, the first television advertisement is usually seen as Eisenhower's 1952 'I like Ike', which featured endorsements from the average American. Since then the use of advertising, particularly in the US, has spiralled from campaign to campaign. The scale of increase in use and sophistication is evidenced on how much is spent. When in 1970, political advertising was first identified as a separate category $12 million

political communication

147

was spent on it in the US, in 2002 it was close to $700 million – the greater use in the 2004 presidential election campaign may well see a further increase.

There are three types of advertising employed by political candidates: advocacy, comparative and negative. Early advertisements such as 'I like Ike' highlighted the qualities of Eisenhower the man and why he should be president, advertising provided a forum for offering competing images and the public were able to decide from these and other appearances, such as the fabled live public debates, who was the best man for the job. However, as pure advocacy began to fail, candidates began to think of ways of attacking their opponent in an advertisement, resulting in the contrast or issue advertisement where both candidates were compared on an issue and the sponsor, naturally, was given favourable spin. Negative advertisements simply focus on the opponent; usually these are justified and open up the campaign to rebuttal and counter-rebuttal. Dolan (in Schultz, 2004) separates out 'Attack Ads' as a separate character. Though they are purely negative, these are deceptive and aggressive, they will identify weaknesses such as voting against a popular policy in the Senate but take it out of context. **Negativity**, and particularly the further blurring of the boundary between justified and deceptive attacks, are commonplace in the US, a feature that is spreading elsewhere though few other nations use the amount of paid-for television spots as American candidates.

Political advertising uses all forms of media; in the US paid-for television spots are the most common. Elsewhere parties and candidates rely on free media access and then pay for billboard posters, magazine advertisements or direct mail flyers. At the local level, the window poster or garden sign remain a feature of electioneering; however, the majority of studies argue that it is the national dimension of an **election campaign**, and so the mass advertising, that has the greatest effect.

KEY FEATURES

Arthur Sanders (2004), an expert in the use of advertising and the media in the US, argues that successful political advertisements should exhibit four features. They should:

1 have dramatic impact, to ensure interest and aid recall;
2 draw on familiar themes, stories and genres to appear relevant;
3 focus on people, often real people and not politicians or actors, rather than policy;
4 be simple, so carrying one easily understood message.

These factors, if combined correctly and adjusted for the context of the campaign in which they are to be used, should ensure that the advertisement offers the most important quality: credibility. If the advertisement's message, or the messenger, lacks credibility, then the voter will dismiss it as just an advertisement, another piece of the diet of slick salesmanship that the modern media audience faces.

The trend in political advertising is towards negativity. While this must be used as part of a campaign that offers positive messages regarding a party or candidate, negative advertisements are said to attract more interest, receive higher recall and have a greater impact; however, they are also argued to turn off the voters from politics. Thus the role of advertising and what styles are appropriate for politics are hotly contested, particularly within studies of modern US political communication and with regard to the Americanisation of campaigning.

THE ACADEMIC AND PRACTICAL DEBATES

There are three key debates regarding political advertising. The first relates to the effects of negativity; the second to the lack of ethical regulation; and the third to the lack of spending controls. If we take negativity first, it is argued that the bombardment of the public with negative or attacking messages actually turns them away from the political system, that it damages the public sphere and reduces civic engagement. The game of rebuttal and counter-rebuttal leaves the audience, and especially the floating voter, confused over what is the truth and so they reject the concept of voting in the spirit of 'a curse on both your houses'. This, it is argued, is most common in the US where choice is limited; both candidates spend vast amounts on a sophisticated campaign, and use more negative messages than any other democracy.

The disengagement thesis is reinforced by evidence that a large proportion of advertising content is actually false. For example, in one famous US advertisement George Bush, Snr. attacked his opponent Michael Dukakis over the controversial and unpopular furlough programme. This policy allowed convicted prisoners time with their families, and had been very successful until one convict, Willie Horton, went on a rampage of kidnapping, rape and torture. Dukakis was blamed for the policy because he was Governor of Maryland, the state where the policy was in place. However, the policy was actually that of his predecessor, a Republican, though Dukakis was supportive of the policy and had done nothing to reverse it. The advertisement, however, placed all responsibility with Dukakis, telling the audience that

'America can't afford the risk' of a Dukakis presidency. Opponents of the deceptive tactics call for regulation; in fact, in Australia, Senator Murray, a Democrat, put forward a 'Political Honesty' bill to end such practices.

Finally, critics argue that the spending is out of control. Using the US as a benchmark, Sally Young (2004) argues that Australian politicians are obsessed with advertising with governments spending $A160 million in a non-election year. Young supports notions that the public feel they are being deceived, and that the use of deception is inherently damaging to democracy.

So, can there be a case for the use of advertising? The answer is affirmative, and that it should be underpinned by raising interest and awareness. Advocates argue that entertaining advertisements are the only way of reaching the voter, basically if it does not look like popular culture and have a dramatic theme voters will switch off.

Interestingly in France, where political advertisements have been banned for the last decade, the recent low turnout in the primaries and appearance of neo-fascist Jean-Marie Le Pen in the run-off, have led to discussions on reconnecting the public with politics. The solution is advertising. Research by political analysts Ipsos argue that the majority of people would be in favour of the reintroduction of political advertising, though the simplicity of the question does not consider how aware they may be of what this would constitute. However, the report also argues that advertising would have benefits for the efficacy of the system. Examples of the carnival atmosphere created by billboards promoting PASOK and the New Democracy parties in Greece highlight that interest can be earned through self-promotion. Equally, a previously unpopular candidate, Spain's Jose Luis Rodriguez Zapatero, was able to create 'a sense of friendliness and energy' as opposed to his previous image of appearing 'aloof and dull' (Ipsos, 2004). Ipsos argue that borrowing the example of these nations would aid French President Chirac to learn 'a new political language' that will reconnect him to the lives of everyday people.

Perhaps the debate here centres on extremes. At one end we have the US and Australian model of high spending and high attack, at the other in nations like Spain and Greece with emergent democratic traditions, democracy is celebrated. Clearly the latter seems more efficacious, but advertising is born of that context also. The US tradition is more adversarial, has only two competitors, each with a high budget, and so every medium is used to promote oneself and attack your opponent. Clearly, then, the effect on the publics will be different, therefore we may conclude that it is the way advertising is used, the level of negativity and the level of deception, as well as the political context, that makes it a good or bad feature of a campaign.

FURTHER READING

The rules of successful advertisements is explored by A. Sanders (2004) 'Creating effective political ads', in David A. Shultz (ed.), *Lights, Camera, Campaign: Media, Politics and Political Advertising*. New York: Peter Lang. pp. 1–20. The role of negativity is explored in a US context by Ansolabehere and Iyengar (1997) *Going Negative*. New York: Free Press in a UK context by J. Dermody and R. Scullion (2002) 'Perceptions of negative political advertising. Meaningful or Menacing?', *International Journal of Advertising*, 19 (2): 201–23; and in an Australian context by Sally Young (2004) *The Persuaders: Inside the Hidden Machine of Political Advertising*. Melbourne: Pluto. Shultz's (2004) collection *Lights, Camera, Campaign: Media, Politics and Political Advertising*, represents the most recent exploration of the role of political advertising and its relationship with media management and places it within the context of a campaign rather than being an abstract element. The report by Ipsos (2004) is part of a special edition of *Ipsos Ideas*, 2 (2), October on political advertising entitled The Faces of Political Seduction and is available from www.ipsos.com/ideas

— Political Marketing —

> *Political marketing refers to the use of marketing tools, concepts and philosophies within the field of policy development, campaigning and internal relations by political parties and organisations. It is seen as a reaction to the rise of political consumerism, and the collapse of partisanship, in western democratic societies as well as emergent democracies.*

151

Ever since Downs (1957) discussed the sovereignty of consumer culture in his *Economic Theory of Democracy*, there have been studies of the similarities and differences between our consumption of a range of consumer goods and of political outputs. Kotler and Levy (1969) noted the fact that political candidates are 'marketed as well as soap'; however, more recent work has progressed to focus on the role of marketing in the stages of policy design and applying what are known as the 4Ps of marketing: product, promotion, place and price. Product equates to policy, party and image, including the tangible and intangible aspects. Promotion and place refer to the design and delivery of the communicational aspects. Price, though less applicable, relates to the transaction of the vote which, normatively, is exchanged for a party carrying out the promises it communicated (Wring, 2004).

The driving force behind the adaptation of marketing to politics is linked to the phenomenon of **dealignment** that has forced parties to move from simply offering their 'product', what some refer to as the 'offering', and relying on this to be wanted by the voter, to selling themselves in a similar way to fast-moving consumer goods. As more parties use increasingly sophisticated techniques of salesmanship, so the competitive edge is lost, leading them to proceed to what is referred to as a market orientation; they allow the market, or electorate, power to design parts of the product. This conception of a market orientation, is distinct from the corporate concept of a marketing orientation where marketing becomes the central philosophy, which would be inappropriate for a political organisation as there is more to their operation than the management of a brand and a single set of products. Parties must also govern, which means determining the right course for a nation long term and not pandering to short-term goals in the name of quick profits. The evolution of political parties is depicted in Table 3.

As part of **professionalisation**, and particularly **Americanisation**, political marketing underpins many of the recent developments of political communication. With it demanding that political actors offer that which the voters desire (or need), politicians use tools such as **image** creation through **aestheticisation** and **emotionalisation**, the appearance of **authenticity**, and relevance and **segmentation** of the electorate to target messages. It can also, however, mean degradation to **populism** providing policy is not developed with any real understanding of long-term, rather than short-term, needs.

Table 3 *Political marketing orientations*

Orientation	Communication mode	Strategic tools	Communication targets
Production	Propaganda	Exposure	Voters
Sales	Media	Market research Market segmentation Advertising/Public relations	Voters
Market	Political marketing	Market Research Policy development Positioning Market segmentation Advertising/Public relations Direct mail	Voters Members Affiliates Donors Mass media Opinion formers

Source: adapted from Shama, 1976

KEY FEATURES

As noted, there are two factors driving the use of political marketing: first, are the trends towards political disloyalty and political consumerism among the electorate; second, is the need to retain a competitive edge over electoral challengers. Parties meet these by going through a number of strategic stages, all of which are geared towards the electoral cycle. While these stages may not be discrete and non-contiguous in reality, it is useful to separate out the orientations and the stages that each type of party go through for ease of understanding. Figure 11 shows the Lees-Marshment model derived from a comparative study of political parties (Lilleker and Lees-Marshment, 2005).

The key to market orientation as presented in Figure 11 are stages 1, 3 and 4. The use of market intelligence to design party behaviour, so to gain a competitive edge, is the fundamentally new aspect that market orientation introduces to politics. Party behaviour will include the leader, for example the construction of the image of UK Prime Minister Tony Blair; party policy and promises, as developed for the New Zealand Labour Party prior to the 2002 general election; or what is becoming known as the party's brand image. The latter is key to establishing an image of competence, but is difficult to change, yet a diverse array of parties and candidates have rebranded themselves in line with voter opinion. Some examples would be Brazil's APRA, formerly a radical revolutionary party now looking to be the party of government after the

political communication

153

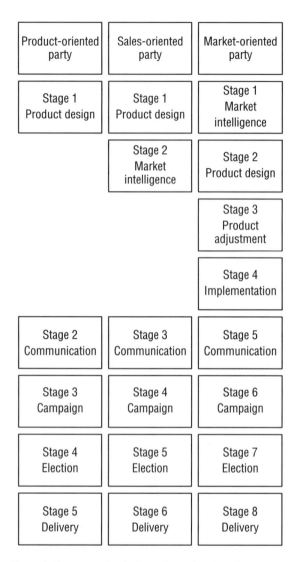

Product-oriented party	Sales-oriented party	Market-oriented party
Stage 1 Product design	Stage 1 Product design	Stage 1 Market intelligence
	Stage 2 Market intelligence	Stage 2 Product design
		Stage 3 Product adjustment
		Stage 4 Implementation
Stage 2 Communication	Stage 3 Communication	Stage 5 Communication
Stage 3 Campaign	Stage 4 Campaign	Stage 6 Campaign
Stage 4 Election	Stage 5 Election	Stage 7 Election
Stage 5 Delivery	Stage 6 Delivery	Stage 8 Delivery

Figure 11   *The marketing process for product, sales and market-oriented parties*

2006 election; the Republic of Ireland's Sinn Fein, as it moves away from its terrorist past and builds a nationalist socialist agenda there are clear increases in support in both Northern Ireland and the Republic; and the USA's George W. Bush who beat Al Gore in 2000 in part by launching himself as a compassionate conservative Republican, rather than the candidate of the 'rich and white Texan'.

Stages 3 and 4 are highly important as rebranding clearly changes the behaviour of the party. Adjustment looks at four key elements: achievability, internal reaction, competition analysis and support analysis. Simply put, can that which the new image promises be delivered, will it divide the party, does it differentiate the party from its competitors, will it lose the party support among the loyal. It is argued that the APRA, Sinn Fein and Bush have been successful here, so far, UK's New Labour less so as it has lost supporters who see it as too close to the Conservative Party politically. While this could be a problem in the adjustment, it could also indicate a failure in implementation. Party members and supporters may well agree to changes in the name of electoral success; however, they may assume the changes are purely cosmetic. Thus if a rebranding strategy is only conducted around the leadership, not through all elements of a mass party, there will clearly be conflict as each section pulls in opposite directions. This may not be a problem for the first election campaign; however, subsequent campaigns may witness division, low turnout among supporters and general dissatisfaction for a 'product' that did not live up to expectations.

Communication is important to the success of a market-oriented party, and should feature a number of key elements. It should:

- be like any other organisation's marketing strategy, centralised, professional and uniform;
- be directed internally as well as externally, both selling the new direction of the party;
- stress competence and image above policy, as the latter should be known desires of the voters;
- feature branded symbols that have resonance with the voter, for example a picture of the leader/candidate, party logo, key messages;
- be both broadcast to the masses and narrowcast to target segments through key media modes;
- be designed and tested through strategic market intelligence;
- be ongoing, and not limited purely to periods of election campaigning.

THE ACADEMIC AND PRACTICAL DEBATES

Political marketing is a phenomenon that has become controversial on both practical and normative grounds. A key issue for both aspects is the role of the public in designing aspects of party behaviour, and in particular, policy. In practical terms, because much policy development is a secretive process, it is difficult to identify the role of market intelligence. Lilleker and Negrine (2005) argue that much intelligence is used for salesmanship, rather than having input into design, and that even those involved in the policy development process are unclear of the extent to which the public voice is heard. This, however, may stem from the Burkean tradition that exists among the political elite. Traditionally, politics is an elite activity, conducted by those who know best on behalf of the masses: to relinquish control is to negate their own role in the political process. Therefore many politicians, when interviewed, are hostile to the notion of marketing concepts and reject suggestions of parties becoming market-oriented. While this is not uniform, and some politicians and strategists highlight the importance of being, or at least being seen to be, market-led, evidence suggests there are divisions over the use of marketing. Evidence from the research of O'Cass (2001) in Australia, and Lilleker and Negrine (2005) in the UK, show there are elements of a marketing philosophy that are adopted, but that it is difficult to identify any party with a pure market orientation.

However, it is also questioned whether such a strategy is correct anyway. Politics, to some, is about ideology and values: to follow public opinion, however strategic the collection, leaves a party rudderless, constantly shifting at the mercy of knee-jerk reactions. While market intelligence suggests the areas of importance, and ideology can suggest the political response, it is noted that marketing draws parties to the centre ground, that which is occupied by the non-aligned or floating voter. Thus parties are difficult to differentiate from one another, and voter engagement is reduced.

There are also broad questions, raised elsewhere, regarding the communicational aspects: aestheticisation and emotionalisation, spin, packaging, designer politics, all of which are described as being the result of parties using marketing. While these are heralded and criticised equally, it is difficult to determine where the advantages lie for parties. Yet as voters become increasingly volatile in their electoral choices, and parties seek increasingly sophisticated methods of reaching out to the electorate, it seems that marketing will be used more and more. At each election more consultants are introduced into the political arena, what Wring (1991) describes as a colonisation of politics, each one bringing ideas from the corporate environment. Thus it seems that political marketing is to have a long history, despite the questions regarding its appropriateness.

FURTHER READING

The earliest study is P. Kotler and S. Levy (1969) 'Broadening the concept of marketing'. *Journal of Marketing*, 33 (1): 54–9; see also A. Shama (1976) 'The marketing of political candidates', *Journal of the Academy of Marketing Science*, 4 (4): 767–77. More recent studies include D. Lilleker and J. Lees-Marshment (2005) *Political Marketing: A Comparative Perspective*. Manchester: Manchester University Press; A. O'Cass (2001) 'An investigation of the political marketing concept and political market orientation in Australian politics,' *European Journal of Marketing*, 35 (9/10): 1003–25; D. Wring (2004) *The Politics of Marketing the Labour Party*. Basingstoke: Palgrave. For a more critical approach to the discussion see D. Lilleker and R. Negrine (2005) 'Mapping a market-orientation: Can we only detect political marketing through the lens of hindsight?', in P.J. Davies and B. I. Newman, *When Elections are on the Horizon: Marketing Politics to the Electorate in the USA and the UK*. New York: Haworth. On the use of consultants see D. Wring (1999) 'Marketing's colonization of politics', in B.I. Newman (ed.) *Handbook of Political Marketing*. Thousand Oaks, CA: Sage.

Popular Culture

At the basic level, popular culture is what is in vogue, that which is popular among a majority of the people. This would include television genres, film, music, fiction or even ideas; it is usually contrasted with 'high' culture, which is seen to appeal to an elite.

political communication

ORIGINS AND LINKS

157

Popular culture is argued to be founded in commercial consumption, it is that which sells as opposed to that which appeals to a minority and is the result of creative genius. Clearly this dichotomy is challenged in comedy and popular music and by the fact that there is a blurring between that which is high culture and that which is popular: for example opera singers such as Pavarotti have made the transition to popular culture. The problem is that becoming associated with popular culture suggests **populism**, a **dumbing down** of the associated art and, in a political communication context, seen as part of a culture of designer politics.

KEY FEATURES

It is argued that the boundaries between popular culture and politics are becoming increasingly blurred. Evidence for this is founded on political actors placing themselves within popular culture contexts to increase their appeal. There are many examples of this phenomenon, some introduced elsewhere in this text, but we would highlight Nicolas Sarkozy's courting of chat show hosts and appearances on French television, Clinton playing saxophone on *The David Letterman Show* or the appearance in 1985 of UK Labour leader Neil Kinnock in a pop video alongside comedienne Tracy Ullmann. These attempts at humanisation of the politician, to show the 'man' or 'woman' behind the suit, are seen as important in an age where the public seem largely disengaged from electoral politics.

However, it is not solely a case of politicians appearing out of context. Popular culture can play a role in framing political discourse. US television drama *The West Wing* depicts a heroic president besieged by manipulative spin-doctors, divisive underlings and a hostile media, yet he still saves the world on a weekly basis while remaining a man of the people. The Clinton-esque connotations are obvious, but also the programme can offer a positive view of the office of the president and the efficacy of the US political system. This is contrasted in the UK television drama *Spooks*, where MI5 are shown as pawns of a manipulative, sometimes corrupt and sleazy government, with hints offered that this is the Blair government. Popular culture can also be used to change public perceptions. UK soap opera *EastEnders* deliberately introduced a popular, but HIV positive, character played by former child actor Todd Carty. The creation of a heterosexual character with AIDS, and showing his battles against prejudice, reinforced government information about the low danger of catching AIDS without engaging in sexual intercourse.

Celebrities also transcend the popular culture/political divide. Bono is world famous as an activist as well as being lead singer of U2; Bob Geldof's campaigning for writing off Third World debt, and organisation of Band Aid in 1984 and Live 8 in 2005, cemented his global profile; while Stevie Wonder's evergreen, and seemingly apolitical, pop hit 'Happy

Birthday' was written to be the backdrop of the campaign for a celebration of Martin Luther King Day. It is also argued that underground music in East Germany exacerbated the fall of the Berlin Wall, such is the power bestowed on popular culture; but is this power used wisely?

THE ACADEMIC AND PRACTICAL DEBATES

John Street (1995) argues that popular culture is not able to change politics, or our perceptions of politics, the audience do not decode popular culture for those cues. Rather it is able to 'articulate the feelings and passions that drive politics' (p. 191). It is able to provide a humanising format for politicians to show that they are authentic, 'of the people', sharing their needs, concerns and fears and that they possess ideas grounded in reality. Clearly this is important in a postmodern political context. However, does this dumb down politics, or is dumbing down actually about making it relevant and so cannot be such a bad thing anyway? It seems the latter is increasingly being seen as true.

Some argue that popular culture actually distracts the audience from what is important. In a Marxist tradition, with television replacing religion as the opium of the masses, some argue that popular culture actually reinforces the hegemony of ideas, controlling the public sphere by imbibing civic society with apolitical concepts. While this argument can be seen as relevant to the case of *The West Wing*, clearly Michael Moore's film *Fahrenheit 9/11* challenges that hegemony, as does the UK's *Spooks* or the political satire enjoyed in most nations.

Others raise concerns about the participation of celebrities in political activism. While some, like Marshall (1997), argue that celebrities can be more representative or 'in touch' with the public mood than elected politicians, others detract from this perspective. While there may be an 'affective' or emotional connection between a celebrity and their fans, this connection could be exploited for political influence. In simple terms, celebrities may use the power they gain from success in one area of popular culture to influence other areas of social life. While this may be the case we could also highlight that there is no evidence to suggest adverse effects of celebrity contribution to political discourse, one could claim that actually audiences may choose to support a celebrity's political stance or reject it on the basis of how it fits our own reading of the issues. Just because high-profile individuals such as Bono, Bob Geldof or Bruce Springsteen, or even the mass of rock bands that are said to have contributed to the velvet revolution in eastern Europe during the late 1980s, promote a cause, there is no evidence to suggest fans will follow their lead.

political communication

159

FURTHER READING

An excellent study is John Street (1995) *Politics and Popular Culture*. Oxford: Polity; see also P.D. Marshall (1997) *Celebrity and Power: Fame in Contemporary Culture*. London: University of Minnesota Press. For a full debate see J. Street (2004) 'Celebrity politicians: Popular culture and political representation', *British Journal of Politics and International Relations*, 6 (4): 435–52.

> *Populism in theory is appealing to that which is the popular or majoritarian opinion. However, normally it is used to denote appeals to nationalist or base opinion, opinion without social conscience.*

ORIGINS AND LINKS

Populism has a long legacy; however, it was first explored in relation to the rise of fascism in the 1930s in Germany, Italy and the UK. It remains intrinsically linked to right-wing, nationalist ideals. More recently, parties using **political marketing** have been accused of populism, due to the focus on public opinion when setting political priorities; however, this is largely an erroneous critique. While parties may develop popular promises, these are largely informed by more than base opinion, hence we see welfare policy, the economy, or unemployment placed on the agenda. Populism can only produce short-term gains, electorally or socially, long-term it is seen as counter-productive. Populist communication is **propagandist** and **rhetorical**, and can draw on **emotionalisation** and **authenticity**.

KEY FEATURES

Populist appeals, normally, will follow a similar format:

- Appeals will focus on concepts of nationhood and national identity.
- Threats to the nation will be used as a focus for unity.
- Promises will be extreme, radical but not costed.
- Populism will draw heavily on symbolism, images of a mythical past and figures, and imagery that unifies.

Parties or candidates that are wholly populist tend not to enjoy substantial electoral success, but can be a threat when the main parties appear too similar, lack appeal or are mistrusted.

Populist candidates would include radical and extrovert Dutch politician Pim Fortuyn and Danish Peoples Party leader Carl Kagan, both of whom threaten the established parties and can raise issues such as immigration onto the political agenda but are excluded from office. However, neo-fascist Jorg Haider was able to win power in Austria. As Lederer et al. (2005) argue, the lack of a clear and practical programme, beyond repatriation of non-Austrians, meant they were unable to govern. Haider's charisma sustained the party for a short time, impotency forced his resignation and the party collapsed. His authoritarian style and promise of power worked only until the election result, demonstrating the emptiness of populist appeals.

THE ACADEMIC AND PRACTICAL DEBATES

The key question asked is whether populism is now more of an anomaly, the preserve of marginal parties and organisations that have no realistic chance of gaining power except under exceptional circumstances. For the most part few parties rely completely on populist appeals; rather they tend to be woven into a political programme. Immigration has become an issue across western Europe, parties that weave anti-immigration policies into their programme have enjoyed greater electoral success than those that omit it from the agenda or propose a liberal stance. Similarly, appeals to populist images of sovereignty, nationhood and national particularism are prevalent in debates on the European Union in Denmark, Norway and the UK. The problem with populism is that it constrains debate; as such appeals aim at subconscious emotions, rather than logic or objectivity. Thus, while successful in certain contexts, populism is regarded in academia as debasing and dumbing down debate, a mode of communication incompatible with modern democracy despite the fact that it is still a feature of much party political communication.

political communication

An excellent introduction to populism and a case study of a populist party can be found in A. Lederer, F. Plasser and C. Scheucher (2005) 'The rise and fall of populism in Austria: A political marketing perspective', in D.G. Lilleker and J. Lees-Marshment (2005) *Political Marketing in Comparative Perspective*. Manchester: Manchester University Press. pp. 132–47. See also C. Calhoun (1988) 'Populist politics, communications media and large scale societal integration', *Sociology*, 6: 219–41.

Propaganda

> *Propaganda is communication that is deliberately designed by one group in society to influence the attitudes and behaviour of others. It often uses symbolism and rhetoric and appeals to the emotional and irrational aspects of our sensibility.*

ORIGINS AND LINKS

Propaganda is, perhaps, the oldest form of political communication that remains today. It remains far more widely used than many scholars or political actors like to admit. The term derives from the Latin name for an organisation set up by the Roman Catholic Church in 1622 to fight the rise of Protestantism. This organisation propagated fears that protestants would burn in the eternal fires of hell for rejecting Catholicism; interestingly the language used to put forward the case for the 'War on Terror' by US President George W. Bush and UK Prime Minister Tony Blair is seen to parallel such activities. However, propaganda is not simply about promoting fights between good and evil in an atmosphere of fear. Propaganda, though more associated with totalitarian regimes, arguably underpins much 'government information' in the 21st century.

Since the use of propaganda as a form of social control by the Catholic

Church, the regimes of Stalin, Hitler, Pol Pot and numerous other dictators, it has highly negative associations. However, it is now subsumed into the work of **political advertising**, **permanent campaigning** and the **public relations state** and is evidenced through the continued use of **spin** and **news management**. Its use reinforces the **hegemonic model** of the **public sphere**, increasing **cynicism** and disengagement from the political process due to its undermining of the pluralist democratic process.

KEY FEATURES

Because propaganda is a term that few are willing to use as a descriptor for political communication, we are not always aware of the extent to which we who live in pluralist democracies are faced with propagandist messages. However, as all political communicators engage in news management and agenda-setting strategies, clearly they add spin to their stories in order to receive coverage. If that spin is reported verbatim, depending often on editorial control, then we are subject to the will of the propagandist. But this would be a rather simplistic definition of propaganda: condemning all communication that contains persuasive elements. At the heart of true propaganda are three key elements: rhetoric, myth and symbolism. Propaganda tends to use all of these to talk to our base emotional impulses, the myth and symbolism of the British Empire or the German Reich are often used by far-right nationalist groups. Equally, we find the rhetoric of death and destruction, the distortion of facts and symbolic representations of nature central to the campaigns of environmentalist and anti-poverty organisations. Often it is common for us to condemn the messages we dislike, those of racist, misogynistic or terrorist groups, but allow the messages we support to permeate our subconsciousness.

Therefore we need to identify the use of rhetoric, symbolism and myth within communications, such as party press releases, before we decide that they are acting as propagandists. However, some would argue that all forms of direct communication are designed to influence the audience (O'Shaughnessy, 2004). They create fictional realities that the audience is meant to believe in, and believe are the result of acting in a particular way: for example, voting for the party, donating to a cause, becoming an activist. Propaganda, however, must follow certain rules. It:

- seeks to draw the reader into and beyond the text, causing internal conflict over issues or reinforcing prejudices we often like to deny we possess: racism particularly;

political communication

163

- highlights that change is possible through action by the reader, comparing negative aspects of the past to a positive future as a result of the action;
- conveys the impression of being objective truth, unsponsored and coming from the public sphere rather than attempting to influence the audience;
- treats the audience as passive, there is no hint that the audience can use differential decoding to block out parts of a message and so not be motivated to act;
- is overt in using visual, rhetorical and symbolic tools, but those must belong to society and be simply and universally decoded as the originator intends.

THE ACADEMIC AND PRACTICAL DEBATES

Many scholars highlight the role of propaganda within the communication of political actors (Moloney, 2001; Rampton and Stauber, 2003). They highlight the dangers to pluralist democracy, the freedom of the media, and the strength of civic culture, all of which seem to enforce the notion of a passive, uncritical audience.

However, conversely we are told that the postmodern audience is anything but passive. That audience members only accept that which we are predisposed to believe, or see as relevant; hence much advertising and marketing is rejected and with it political propaganda. Equally, audiences decode messages in different ways. While rhetoric of the state or nation may have an effect on those with nationalistic or racist tendencies, others may be put off by such appeals. The use of myths in communication, myths of a future society or world for example, are only accepted if the myth is believed. Some audience members will have access to alternative viewpoints and sources of influence, thus they are able to reject the symbolic communication.

As is the case with the sophisticated tools of advertising and marketing that political communicators use to influence key publics, so a large majority of propagandist appeals are rejected as empty rhetoric. This operates in the same way as when the notion that one brand is 'the best' is rejected without personal evidence of that being the case. Thus the propagandist communicator is unable to convince all of their audience; in fact, it is debatable whether propaganda works on anybody apart from those predisposed to believe the message anyway.

FURTHER READING

A solid overview is provided by N. O'Shaughnessy (2004) *Politics and Propaganda: Weapons of Mass Seduction*. Manchester: Manchester University Press. The use of propaganda is well documented, see K. Moloney (2001) 'The rise and fall of spin: Changes of fashion in the presentation of UK politics', *Journal of Public Affairs*, 1 (2): 124–35; S. Rampton and J. Stauber (2003) *Weapons of Mass Deception: The Uses of Propaganda in Bush's War on Iraq*. New York: Tarcher, the latter looking at US government communication surrounding the 2003 'War on Terror'.

Pseudo-Events

A pseudo-event is an event that takes place purely to gain media and public attention. As such it is a non-event; however, is used to communicate image-related symbolism to the audience.

ORIGINS AND LINKS

The need and desire for politicians, particularly during election campaigns, to be visibly active and in the news, coupled with the requirement for attractive stories by a 24/7 news machine, means that elements of news are manufactured by the politician. The pseudo-event can range from the candidate making an appearance at a real event, paying a visit to an area or key institution, or by making news in more subtle ways. Boorstin (1961) discusses the pseudo-event as a synthetic element of US news culture as early as the 1920s, which journalists would seek out 'to make up for the lack of spontaneous events'.

In the postmodern election campaign they are a key feature designed to communicate **authenticity**. They are a way of **packaging** political messages, such as a politician's concern for health care by visiting a hospital, or law and order by going on the streets with police officers, or appearance alongside celebrities. German Chancellor Schroeder enjoyed appearing with both businessmen and the 'common people' in order to

political communication

165

show he understood the whole of society in the 2002 election campaign: earlier some elements of the media had criticised him for brokering a deal to save Philippe Holzmann's debt-ridden construction group with taxpayers' money then appearing outside Holzmann's Frankfurt headquarters to announce the saving of jobs to hundreds of construction workers. Thus the media may not always handle these events favourably. In contrast, Tarja Halonen, Finland's female president, chose to capture the media spotlight by dancing with soul legend James Brown at the Finnish Jazz Festival; while the media reported this objectively her approval ratings were seen to peak at 94 per cent following the appearance.

KEY FEATURES

Political communication is peppered with pseudo-events, some of media choosing; however, a true politically motivated pseudo-event will:

- be scripted and dramatic;
- be of interest to the media audience;
- produce iconic images: impassioned crowds, celebrities, perhaps the obligatory baby kissing;
- be designed to be reassuring: in one consultant's words 'Even if we cannot discuss intelligently the qualifications of the candidates or the complicated issues, we can at least judge the effectiveness of a television performance';
- create the illusion that we who watch it are 'informed';
- lead to an endless number of other pseudo-events, often staged by opponents competing for media coverage.

While these features are evergreen and would be familiar to any public relations practitioner of the last millennia, political parties particularly have increased the use of pseudo-events and their control over media reporting of them. One example here would be the party conferences and rallies which, once forums for debate, now are stage-managed to ensure that an image of a strong, cohesive party, supportive of the leader, is transmitted to the audience (Stanyer, 2001). Such events can obscure reality, and create problems for journalists attempting to inform rather than purely entertain.

THE ACADEMIC AND PRACTICAL DEBATES

Media journalists raise the greatest concerns about pseudo-events. While forced to cover the activities of electoral candidates, journalists will often be subjected to a staged event that diverts coverage from other, less favourable events or news items. Equally, candidates from opposing organisations will compete for media coverage by staging events to clash with those of their opponents, though at times this can result in the media's refusal to cover either. Hence the concern relates to the fact that the news of pseudo-events can drive out news covering real issues and real events. But is this always the case? Journalists have the power to frame coverage of an event to fit existing news agendas. They also create their own events, often designed to foil the news management strategies of electoral candidates. Thus, while journalists often claim to be slaves to party or government machines, this is rarely a reality (Clarke, 2003).

A more serious point relates to the information subsidy that is provided by the pseudo-event. While they may not be reported, if they are they focus solely on image, symbolism and rhetoric, and largely will say little about substantive political issues. They eschew debate and enforce a contrived view of politics. In Baudrillard's (1993) view they represent a simulation of reality, while not being real. Beneath this umbrella critique he would include the current trends in the reporting of war with cameras attached to SCUD missiles giving the impression of viewing an action movie. Thus, critics argue that the staging of the events, and the complicity of the media in transmitting them, reduce real thought among the audience and stifle political debate; this is replaced by a stupefying range of images that present us with a false reality of life beyond our homes.

FURTHER READING

The seminal text remains Daniel Boorstin (1961) *The Image: A Guide to Pseudo-Events in America.* New York: Vintage. On party events in the UK see James Stanyer (2001) *The Creation of Political News: Television and British Party Political Conferences.* Brighton: Sussex Academic Press. An interesting case study on the withdrawal of Vietnamese troops from Cambodia is offered by Judith Clarke (2003) 'How journalists judge the reality of an international pseudo-event', *Journalism*, 4 (1): 50–75; for a more theoretical account see William Merrin (2002) 'Implosion, simulation and the pseudo-event: a critique of McLuhan', *Economy and Society*, 31 (3): 369–90. See also J. Baudrillard (1993) *Symbolic Exchange and Death.* London: Sage.

political communication

167

Public Relations Democracy

> *Public relations democracy is a term used to describe a pluralist society with a free media and where much of the communication that comes out of the political system is designed to persuade the public that policies are correct, that laws and procedure are legitimate and that one organisation is better at representing groups of voters than its competitors.*

ORIGINS AND LINKS

Where there is a close parallel between a party of government and one or several media organisations, such as the US Republican Party's links to Fox TV or Italian Prime Minister Berlusconi's ownership of several commercial television stations, political communicators have an easy task. They are able to get their message across to the public in the manner, style and in the format they want. It is within nations where there are limited controls over the media, whether through partisanship or legal constraint, that parties and governments must exercise persuasion, first, towards the media and secondly, over the people. Therefore it can be argued that every democracy must use persuasive communication, if not the only way to ensure the public obey laws is by threat of punitive action. However, the term public relations democracy has emerged to describe a situation where all communication has persuasive overtones: that all governmental information is tinged with a party political message, and every statement is designed to say something positive about the messenger.

The majority of studies focus on the UK since the election of Tony Blair as Prime Minister in 1997 (Davis, 2002; Franklin, 2004). While often conflated with the notion of spin or marketing, the differences relate to the fundamentals of public relations. The core aim of public relations is to present an individual or organisation in a positive light, to enhance the public's perception of that individual or organisation and, perhaps but not always, to get the public to do something for that individual or organisation. This means that public relations is about **image** creation and **branding, news management** and **campaigning**, it is not necessarily about legitimising a political system. It is argued, however, that this is the function it is being used for; or rather it is being used to legitimise the power of one party through the various governmental communication channels.

KEY FEATURES

The Chartered Institute of Public Relations' Code of Conduct sets out core functions of public relations. It is useful to introduce them here while relating them to the workings of political communication and particularly the UK's Government Information and Communication Service (GICS) and Central Office of Information (COI). These and subsidiaries are tasked with communicating to the public; thus with them lies the responsibility for projecting the image of the 'state'.

The first observation is that public relations is normally employed to represent a single interest or cause. As hinted above this could be the state; however, it is suggested that actually the state has been redefined to be embodied in the party of government and its leader. It could be argued that in a democracy the elected bodies represent the legitimate parts of the state and should be supreme; however, this ignores the checks and balances that exist within a democratic society. When a single party, by dint of being elected, is able to control communication for its own purpose it could be seen to be an elected dictatorship: as critics remind us Hitler was elected, yet it was persuasive communication that was in part the means that allowed him to take control of far more than simply the legislature. While other groups are able to employ public relations to represent them also, the resources of government enable one group to have the upper hand in reaching the masses through a multiplicity of channels.

Public relations tools are used in order to gain a profit for the individual or organisation being represented. While the concept of profit is alien to the democratic process, clearly the whole concept of **electoral professionalism** and **permanent campaigning** is geared towards maximising support. This links to a further feature which is that public relations enforces a single perception of reality upon its audience, in other words that it will attempt to impose an ideology upon the masses on behalf of the single interest or cause. Again, within a pluralist system, this would be expected; equally the fact that multiple interests and causes all employ public relations means that no single voice is permanently louder than all competitors. However, when related to the government of a nation, it is argued that governmental public relations is able to 'shout the loudest', drowning out the voices of competitors, and so the incumbent gains an unfair, and perhaps undemocratic, advantage.

Public relations also deals with the world of appearances, not with the world of fact. While we can argue that the promotion of style and image has few negative consequences in the context of an election campaign, and that it is indeed necessary, critics posit that such a trend leads to a restriction of access to real information. Franklin (2004: 90–5) uses the example of the launch of the UK's National Year of Reading in 1998 to highlight the insidious use of public relations tools to present a perception of the government. The then Education Secretary David Blunkett embedded storylines into popular dramas, such as *EastEnders* and teen favourite *Hollyoaks*, while taking part in stunts with the stars of the programmes designed to boost the image of himself and his government as well as the policy. In spite of the fact that this could be seen as a worthwhile venture, given the levels of illiteracy that exist in the UK, the dual promotional purpose led to critics describing the campaign as propagandistic because of the partisan messages contained within the messages. The policy was clearly 'New Labour's', it was personalised by Blunkett's appearance and presented figures to suggest that the problem had not been addressed by the previous Conservative administration. Therefore it reinforced party perceptions, blending fact with a political message: projecting a biased appearance that had party political overtones.

Therefore, within a public relations democracy, we would expect to see a vast amount of governmental communication that promotes the party elected to govern, designed to earn that party future support through promoting its ideology and political programme, and every policy launch will include overtly political messages embedded amongst the facts. There are many instances of such practices, ranging from the German Green Party's attempts to claim ownership of environmental policies through the speeches of their leader Joschka Fischer to flamboyant Dutch politician Pym Fortuyn's arguments that were clearly aimed at image enhancement. However, Tony Blair is seen as the master of the public relations democracy due to the centrality of such promotional tools to New Labour's political programme.

The norm is to argue that such practices are wrong, they are anti-democratic, reduce civic participation and lead to an inactive public sphere and create a cynical public disengaged from the democratic process. Yet they continue to be used. We may well argue that normatively, or in an ideal world, governments should quite simply inform and never ever attempt to persuade the public. But would that work? Certainly it would allow the media the opportunity to control the agenda completely, attach their own spin to a story and control public perceptions through their own partisan bias. This would be countered if we had free, objective and impartial news organisations, but few nations have, and those who claim to often have flaws. Thus few live in a utopia where persuasion is unnecessary; if they existed we may also not need laws, punishment, even elections, as everybody would be serving one another in society.

Realists argue that much of what is referred to as public relations is actually weak propaganda: communication with conviction. As Kevin Moloney (2004) argues, it is all about self-presentation for attention and advantage, it is unashamedly self-interested; but it is also a necessity for any group in power or wishing to attain power. Why then is it necessary if it is anti-democratic? First, it is important to note that the critics seem to offer a linear effects model for political communication; it is transmitted, it is accepted, it is acted upon. Yet this is not the case, the best and worst public relations stunt must have been the September 2003 'dodgy dossier' making the case for war against Iraq. It is almost certain that few accept any part of that document to be true; the reason for this is the accelerated pluralism that mediates against the acceptance of any one propaganda message.

Accelerated pluralism describes a situation where no piece of communication goes uncontested. The fact that each individual audience member has the power to decode a message, process and evaluate it in relation to their personal experiences and ideology and then choose to accept or reject its logic, automatically suggests there is no unitary voice. There may well be voices that are 'louder', yet healthy cynicism means they do not always get attention and are disbelieved in the same way as the words of the opinionated man or woman in the bar, queue or classroom are shrugged off as uninformed ramblings.

However, this does not mean that the use of public relations is not damaging to the democratic process. Neither does it mean there are no alternative uses of public relations. The symmetrical model of

political communication

171

communications suggests a form of democracy where public and political spheres have a communicative synergy; they talk to one another and so persuasion is two-way and decisions are made with the public. This suggests a revised version of public relations democracy that is hotly contested in terms of its practicability. At present such notions are an ideal, a chimera, which some scholars argue are required in order that the public feel represented and perceive power as being exercised legitimately; this cannot happen if all communication is weak propaganda and thus it is argued that new forms of communication are necessary, that political organisations need to bypass the media gatekeepers and open a dialogue with the public.

FURTHER READING

On the current use of public relations see A. Davis (2002) Public Relations Democracy: *Public Relations, Politics and the Mass Media in Britain*. Manchester: Manchester University Press; B. Franklin (2004) *Packaging Politics: Political Communications in Britain's Media Democracy*. London: Arnold. A critique of the relationship between public relations and democracy can be found in K. Moloney (2004) 'Democracy and public relations', *Journal of Communication Management*, 9 (1): 89–92.

Public Sphere

> *The public sphere is an abstract conception of the arena in which debate occurs; it is a hypothetical space which we all inhabit, generating and sharing ideas, where social knowledge is created and where public opinion is constructed. It is any place where people meet, share and discuss ideas and so influence one another.*

172

ORIGINS AND LINKS

Jurgen Habermas, a Marxist scholar, developed the concept of the public sphere, and explored it in depth in *The Structural Transformation of the Public Sphere* (Habermas, 1992). Recognising the flaws in Karl Marx's notion that society would automatically reform itself, through constant upheaval and the internal contradictions of capitalism, towards a more socialist and equal communist existence, Habermas attempted to construct a way to understand how society could influence itself and the political system. Sharing Marx's belief in the inequalities in a representative democracy, he identifies that the public are able to construct alternative conceptions of the future and as these become popularised so society shifts to suit. Habermas, therefore, wrote of the public sphere as 'a network for communicating information and points of view' (1992); it allows the public to communicate with one another and so construct joint opinion.

In the context of a pluralist democracy, communication is seen as crucial to the health of civic society. Thus freedom of speech and expression, and freedom to dissent, is seen as an inalienable right of any member of a democratic society; accordingly, debates on the US Patriot Act and numerous other anti-terrorism measures introduced post 9/11 are often framed in a battle over these freedoms. Their existence, along with a healthy, strong and open public sphere, helps to protect us from the effects of **propaganda**, **negativity** and modern **campaigning** and **political marketing** techniques. While the public sphere may well be highly critical of political leaders or the system in general, this **cynicism** is often regarded as healthy. It represents evidence that the public sphere is active, that there are alternative views being popularised.

The conception of the public sphere is most often applied within media studies. The media, it is argued, in the majority of democratic nations, act along democratic and representative lines. It is the media that advances pluralism into the public sphere by offering a voice to a range of actors and organisations (Price, 1995). While these include political and corporate voices, they also include public voices: those who represent neither political nor corporate organisations. While there are contesting views on the media contribution to pluralism, clearly the media has a key role in contributing to the construction of the public sphere and influencing public opinion, regardless of debates on media effects (see Dahlgren, 1995).

A recent development in debates surrounding the public sphere is the role of the Internet. It is argued that this is a new public space, one that is beyond national boundaries and so able to circumvent legislation and controls on information. In particular we hear of a new dimension to the public sphere: the blogosphere. As members of societies create Internet-based diaries, formally known as web logs and less formally as blogs, a new

political communication

173

medium has been created for gaining access to the public sphere. Although in relative infancy compared to other forms of mass media, much research is devoted to studying the extent to which the Internet facilitates the reinvention of the public sphere, one that is global in its reach (Rodgers, 2003).

KEY FEATURES

Clearly there is a level of intersection between that which is public and that which is private. If we consider both as two spheres, then we may imagine them as they appear in Figure 12, which also features the other actors: the media. Of course, there are many private spheres, though this is represented by only two, all of which intersect with the public sphere. We give to the public sphere our experiential knowledge, through conversations with family, colleagues and other members of the public; we also contribute through participating in opinion polls, by writing letters to newspapers or by entering into any activity that communicates with the broader public sphere. We literally make parts of ourselves public.

The public sphere, however, also enters the private. Our experiences of daily life construct our personal reality; we build perceptions of things like public services and government provision of welfare. This allows us to decode other elements of the public sphere, such as media reportage and political communication, which can be mediated by our experiential knowledge. Thus the public sphere is best characterised as containing nothing but a collection of competing and contrasting voices. Social pluralism allows many voices into the public sphere; it is the members of society that choose which voices, or what noise, is allowed to permeate each individual's private sphere. This process is largely subconscious; however, communication theory dictates that this is governed by credibility: of the source, of the message itself and of the medium which

174

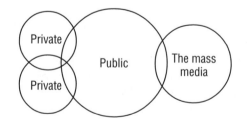

Figure 12   *The process of dealignment (derived from Harrop and Miller, 1987)*

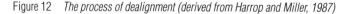

Public Sphere

transmits the message. In a postmodern society, what is credible is based on individual's experiential knowledge: our own interactions with the public sphere throughout our sentient existence.

For a public sphere to be strong, active and open, society must have:

- freedom of speech as a fundamental right;
- a politically independent and pluralist media that is accessible;
- high levels of literacy; including ICT skills;
- open access to government documents.

It is argued that as few societies are perfect in all these respects, then the public sphere is also fundamentally flawed as an independent and influential political force.

THE ACADEMIC AND PRACTICAL DEBATES

Questions surrounding the strength of the public sphere as a force of critical influence usually surround the role of the mass media within pluralist societies (Dahlgren, 1995). As depicted above the mass media certainly enters the public sphere, and has a significant level of influence; however, does it actually constitute the public sphere in the modern age? While the mass media may well be politically independent, or at least sufficient outlets exist to ensure political pluralism, this may not mean that it is universally accessible. Instead, critics argue, the media speaks using the discourse of experts. News values can demote items on the agenda, agenda-setting can prioritise items that are ephemeral, while framing can distract the audience from the importance of a news item; thus information can be presented in a way that subdues activism and promotes an apolitical public sphere. Associated features of media reportage and political communication, such as the packaging of news and policy, dumbing down of news and the aestheticisation and emotionalisation of political discourse, can mean that the public sphere begins to eschew political discourse; or only discuss the ephemera. Thus it is the scandals in political life as well as among celebrities that are discussed by individuals in cafés, public houses and web logs, and political activism is regarded as an irrelevance.

While this gloomy prognosis is far from reality, it is clear that the media has a key role in contributing to the public sphere. If we believe that media effects are limited to telling us what to think about (agenda-setting theory), and if political news is presented in frames of conflict and personalisation (see framing), then that is all the public sphere has to discuss. Critics of

political communication

175

political marketing, arguing that parties lose their differentiation, also highlight this as a cause of de-politicisation of public discourse.

Currently the public are political, though they may show a lower interest in electoral politics than say environmentalism: in fact, political pressure groups are benefiting from the public's lack of interest in supporting parties. This may be deleterious for democratic politics; however, it could also be indicative of the shifting nature of the public sphere. Society, it is argued, is more concerned with causes that effect the individual than with mass politics. An individual's political character may be shaped not along party lines, as was once the case, but is more determined by a combination of their race, religion, financial status, personal security, and life experiences. Therefore it may be the case that this is actually evidence of a new dimension to the public sphere, reflecting the evolution of postmodern society, where politics exists on different levels (Rodgers, 2003). While we have personal concerns, we may also think on a more global level. Thus discussion may focus more on the post 9/11 world order, Third World poverty or, in early 2005, how to contribute to helping the survivors of the Asian tsunami, but have little concern for domestic political debates surrounding which party would be better on welfare policy. If Habermas was right, and the public sphere is a force of political change, perhaps electoral organisations will become equally interested in such issues and the elements that are argued to cause public disengagement, adversarialism and spin, will disappear from democratic political systems.

FURTHER READING

The original and classic text is J. Habermas (1992) *The Structural Transformation of the Public Sphere: Inquiry into a Category of Bourgeois Society*, trans. Cambridge: Polity. On Habermasian theory see C. Calhoun (ed.) (1992) *Habermas and the Public Sphere* (Cambridge, MA: MIT Press); J.M. Roberts and N. Crossley (eds) (2004) *After Habermas: New Perspectives on the Public Sphere*, Sociological Review Monographs. London: Blackwell. On the media's role in the public sphere see P. Dahlgren (1995) *Television and the Public Sphere: Citizenship, Democracy and the Media*. London: Sage; M. Price (1995) *Television, the Public Sphere, and National Identity*. Oxford: Clarendon Press. While not specifically using the language of the public sphere, J. Rodgers (2003) *Spatializing International Politics: Analysing Activism on the Internet*. London: Routledge deals with the new political space offered by the Internet; hence her arguments are highly relevant to rethinking the dimensions of the public sphere.

Representation

Representation is the core concept of democracy. The voters elect an individual or party to act in accordance with their wishes in the running of society. The intrinsic link between voter and representative suggests an open channel of communication facilitates input by both parties that contributes to the legitimisation of the representative democratic system.

ORIGINS AND LINKS

In what manner decisions should be made is at the centre of debates on democracy. The Athenian city state, even with its narrow definition of citizenship and small number of participants, allowed all citizens to engage in collective decision making. However, as populations increased, and national boundaries widened, it is clear that such a system would be unworkable even if it was attractive. As democracy developed it was recognised that some were more intellectually equipped, as well as having more time, to be active in 'affairs of state' than others. It was these elites that became the precursor of today's members of national parliaments. As elite parties evolved into mass parties, it became more important that voters recognised that those they elected would act on their behalf; this would denote the difference between electing a representative and electing a tyrant. Changes in society over the last half decade have increasingly seen the public and political elite become more similar. Not only are politicians often from inauspicious roots, they are equally less likely to be from a minority elite, educated at certain private establishments and have similar social status. While some criticise politicians in western democracies as unrepresentative, self-seeking elites, in reality things are not that bad at all.

However, it is not sufficient that representatives and voters share common social roots; when in power representatives should also do the bidding of the voters in an attempt to serve all society. The member of the national executive should be an agent of the people (Arblaster, 2002), and should not be subservient to any other subgroup within society. In the current age there seems to be an inherent contradiction in the way our democracy works. In the main, voters tend to vote for a political party, each of which have separate ideas, beliefs and political programmes; however, the parties' elected representatives also have their own separate constituencies. Once elected they are expected to represent their constituency, their supporters; if they do not there is little reason for those voters to retain their allegiances. However, this suggests the tyranny of the majority, that if 50 per cent of the electorate vote for one party then, when elected, that party will only cater for the needs of that 50 per cent. As the support of the other 50 per cent is divided among other minority parties then they have little power. Nevertheless, their votes did elect other members of the executive, the opposition parties, so in theory their opinions will be represented, to some extent, within debates in parliament; thus all the people will have some degree of input, via their representatives, to the legislative process.

The concept of representation described above suggests that there must be a channel of communication between the voters and their representatives. In some countries this is possible through the system of having a representative for a geographically defined area. However, it is debatable just how effective this can be. Take the US, for example, where it is open to question whether a Republican governor would be willing or able to represent the wishes of Democrat voters within their state. But communication cannot just take place between disparate members of the legislature and their elected representative. Governments act in the name of their people on a daily basis; hence the slogan of the anti-war campaign in Italy, the US and the UK in 2003 was 'Not In My Name'. In order for people to feel they are being represented effectively then communication must be designed to inform the public why decisions are being made, why the decisions are right in the long term and how their wants and needs are being served.

KEY FEATURES

One would expect that in a system based on representation political marketing would be the norm and, in particular, its emphasis on the constant collection of data that attempts to understand the voter in order to communicate effectively with them. This would not suggest government by focus groups, polling data or even referenda, but maintaining a close link between elected and elector. In contrast, the public often suggest feeling disconnected from the political process and suffering from a mixture of ennui and powerlessness when it comes to considering political communication. It appears that politics is something done to them rather than with them, as the following key indicators of under-representation suggest:

- Electoral volatility and a lack of partisan attachment.
- Declining turnout for electoral contests.
- A lack of political knowledge, particularly among the young.
- Declining levels of trust in established political institutions.
- Declining levels of interest in mainstream political activity.
- Increasing interest in non-electoral political activity.

While these are recognised features of many democracies, do they actually equate to a crisis of representation as is suggested? Some argue they do, and in particular tie this with the decline in civic society and social capital (Putnam, 2001). While this cannot be solved through producing better communication, as is currently being attempted though the adaptation of marketing communication to politics, it may be assuaged by differing uses of communication. So what do we mean by representative, or representational, communication?

At the heart of the concept of representational communication are what Hetherington (1998) describes as representational codes. These are symbolic heuristics, shortcuts that are used in communication to signify common reference points shared within society. These can link to past events, imagined future events, the tangible or the intangible; what they share is that they have a social existence of their own: they mean something to all members of a society. So how does this notion translate into political communication? One such symbol is modernity. This has been deployed by political leaders since the 1960s, and is something we can all imagine but yet is intangible and may all interpret in different ways. It conjures images of being up to date, forward-looking, in touch, competent, the list could go on and on; however, it has an enduring appeal that seems to have some connection with the human psyche.

These representation codes can be linked to presentational codes, acts of expression that convey emotions that are recognised by the audience. It is the recognition that the performer, and we should include the political communicator within that description, is the same as the masses, shares our fears, feelings, etc., which allows the public to also identify with the representational codes used in the speech. Linking these together allow a greater understanding between governed and governors.

However, the political performer is not alone in promoting pluralist representation. Theoretically, the media also promotes pluralism, but adherence to news values and a focus on key target audiences can also mean that marginalized voices go ignored. The representative nature of the media is often questioned, both theoretically and practically. Lumby (1999) in his study of the media shows that there is greater emphasis on entertainment than informing. This means that the audiences are not represented, more diverted. The lack of access to media and political inputs causes a sense of social disconnection; many simply descend into apathy and get on with their own lives mentally insulated from interaction with the state, for others this is not enough. The failure of pluralism leads some political groupings to abandon mainstream communication media and focus on building virtual communities that offer e-representation.

THE ACADEMIC AND PRACTICAL DEBATES

The key question posed by the ideal concept of representation is whether it is possible for a government to represent its entire electorate within the current confines imposed upon political communication. When we discuss the concepts of electoral professionalism, permanent campaigning and the constant aim to gain re-election, can this suggest effective representation? The fear is that all political communication is designed to persuade; but persuasive communication can never be representative.

Arguments to the contrary suggest that the public demand a more aesthetic form of representation. Ankersmit argues that many of the problems that relate to the crisis of representation are caused by the fact that 'the electorate and the state simply are no longer able to recognise and understand one another' (2003: 34). While it may seem tautological that members of a society fail to be recognised and understood simply as a result of them being elected to government, it makes more sense when we consider that it is a failure to understand how to communicate complex issues and decisions to the broader society.

Subgroups in society also feel marginalized and under-, if not unrepresented. Within the US these groups are usually defined by race or economic status, in particular certain ethnic groups in the poorest communities. Campaign communication has been used to attract voters within these groups, for example targeting Spanish language advertising at Latino communities; however, there is no long-term courting of this group. In the UK it seem that young voters feel disconnected, if not alienated, from electoral politics; elsewhere it is gender groups. In the Czech Republic, politics is perceived by female voters as a 'man's club';

they feel under-represented in the composition of parliament as well as by the political outcomes. Often, such under-representation is mirrored within the media.

A further debate is the extent to which such deficits in representation can be solved through access to new media. While much debate focuses on the applications of new technology to e-democracy in an attempt to boost turnout, many researchers suggest that the World Wide Web can also offer a solution to a lack of representation for minority voices. The problem with this is: Will anyone listen to them?

The debates on representation are complex and in many ways age-old. It perhaps goes back to the adage that democracy is far from perfect, but the closest to perfection that we have. Representative democracy has flaws, perhaps because traditions have become entrenched and so a natural separation between the reality of life and the tradition of politics occurs. However, in the eyes of many critics such developments are serious and need reversing. Whether it is communication that is at fault, or whether it can offer remedies is a big question; clearly, however, communication is at the heart of a democratic system of government.

FURTHER READING

For an introduction to democracy and the concept of representation see A. Arblaster (2002) *Democracy*, 2nd edn. Milton Keynes: Open University Press. On the crisis of representation see M. Kaase and K. Newton (1995) *Beliefs in Government*. Oxford: Oxford University Press; R. Putnam (2001) *Bowling Alone*. New York: Simon & Schuster. On the use of aesthetic representation see F. Ankersmit (2003) 'Democracy's inner voice: Political style as unintended consequence of political action', in J. Corner and D. Pels, *Media and the Restyling of Politics*. London: Sage. The representative function of the media is discussed in C. Lumby (1999) *Gotcha! Life in a Tabloid World*. Sydney: Allen and Unwin; a case study of gender representation by the media is offered by H. Havelkova (1999) 'The political representation of women in mass media discourse in the Czech Republic 1990–1998', *Czech Sociological Review*, 7 (2): 145–65.

Rhetoric

> *Rhetoric is the use of symbolism and language to ensure that a message is encoded in the way desired by the communicator. Rhetorical communication is intentionally persuasive, is central to propaganda, and is used to encourage a change in an audience member's behaviour.*

ORIGINS AND LINKS

The use of rhetoric is as age-old as political communication and was seen by Aristotle in his discourses on ancient Greek democratic politics as a necessary means of bending the will of the people. Rhetorical speech is used in all our daily lives, as a means of persuading others, as much as it is a tool common in political communication. It is concerned with ensuring that the interpretation of our message is uniform, at least among a majority. It is central to **campaigning**, underpins **propaganda** and **spin** and is a central form of discourse within the **soundbite culture** of designer politics.

KEY FEATURES

Rhetorical conversation has a key role in a democratic society, it builds consensus by binding the people around ideas and issues. By accepting the logic of rhetoric we belong, it defines our civic duty and encourages participation in order to advance our collective social values; as such, therefore, it dismisses postmodernism as peripheral to underlying social norms and values. Thus rhetorical conversation will have a number of key features. It:

- legitimises, by justifying distribution of power within a social ideology; one can consider here 2004 debates surrounding anti-terrorism laws in the US and the case for ID cards in the UK;
- orients society behind common goals through a narrative of community; this was particularly important for the Danish 'No'

campaign during the referenda on joining the European Monetary Union which was framed in discourses of preserving Danish social benefits, the monarchy and more general issues of sovereignty;

- resolves conflicts through identifying common goals; popular leader of the Norwegian Progressive Party, Svenn Kristiansen, called for the leader of the coalition to resign or offer more power to the NPP, suggesting he would delegitimise the government and force an election. The collective desire to remain in power led to a diplomatic solution;
- mobilises, through activation and organisation. Kristiansen's brinkmanship is one example, as are various political campaigns. For the UK 2005 election, where low turnout was again feared, the Labour slogan 'Britain is working: don't let the Tories ruin it again', was an attempt to mobilise their support and those who feared the Conservatives would undermine Labour's economic policy successes.

To be successful, rhetoric must be designed with a complex understanding of the audience, their social norms, values and fears, and will speak to these directly.

Designers of rhetorical communication thus proceed through a five-stage process. They:

1 identify and define the problem;
2 identify the audience required to solve the problem;
3 identify or infer that audience's interpretive system: their norms, fears and values;
4 translate the problem into the audience's interpretive system: create the message;
5 deliver the message for optimal audience acceptance.

THE ACADEMIC AND PRACTICAL DEBATES

As rhetoric is used by each of us, as well as in corporate advertising and marketing, political organisations and a range of others who would persuade the public, and we are bombarded with different pieces of rhetoric on a daily basis, does it have any effect? Are users of rhetoric kidding themselves when they believe that the public, or any other receiver, believes that failure to act in the way suggested will result in poorer circumstances than those currently experienced. While the logic of postmodernism argues no, clearly rhetoric does work.

The discourse of modernity, using rhetorical terms such as 'new', 'forward-focused' or 'of the people', has been a common campaigning tool for parties excluded from office for protracted periods. The Danish Liberals challenged the 30-year dominance of the Social Democrats through using such rhetorical language, that it was the use of 'modern' and associated terms that was key is reflected by polls. Respondents argued that Liberal leader Anders Fogh Rasmussen fitted the image he had been projecting; he was a modern politician, looking to the long-term future of Denmark and the best for government. The Liberals gained most votes (31.3 per cent) but rely on a coalition with right-wing parties for power. Tony Blair's image and the rebranding of Labour to 'New' Labour has been argued to have created a similar effect, though the subsequent weakness of the competition allowed Labour to form a government with a large majority (Fairclough, 2001).

Campaigning applications of rhetoric intend to mobilise and to promote an image, based within social ideals. However, rhetoric seeking to orient society behind a cause, or mobilise support for or against a policy, can have more divisive effects. The Danish 'NO to EMU' campaign polarised society along normative perspectives: what is society, where are its interests. Similarly, opinions on the US/UK War on Terror have led to accusations of traitorous behaviour being levelled against those who oppose war on Afghanistan and Iraq. While this is the purpose of the rhetoric, to unify a majority behind a cause, it naturally leads to the castigation of social groups; a result incompatible with pluralist democracy. This is the problem with any form of persuasive communication, a problem that is circular in nature. While persuasion is necessary in any pluralist democracy, due to the competitive nature of pluralism, there are always winners and losers. The latter shout foul, complaining of their opponent's media management and spin, in contrast to their reliance on the communication of transparent facts, yet both are forms of rhetorical communication. Hence pluralism and rhetoric become inseparable despite the contradiction in principle.

FURTHER READING

A solid theoretical introduction can be found in Craig A. Smith (1990) *Political Communication*. San Diego: Harcourt Brace Jovanovich. ch. 4; for a somewhat more theoretical and historical review see B.E. Gronbeck (2004) 'Rhetoric and politics', in L. Lee Kaid, *Handbook of Political Communication Research*. London: Lawrence Erlbaum. For a case study of the use by the UK's New Labour see N. Fairclough (2001) *New Labour, New Language?* London: Routledge; numerous examples from both a global and a historic perspective are provided in N. O'Shaughnessy (2004) *Politics and Propaganda: Weapons of Mass Seduction*. Manchester: Manchester University Press.

Segmentation

> *A segmentation strategy is one where the electorate is divided into groups, often based on either sociodemographics or political affiliation, to enable the targeting of communication.*

ORIGINS AND LINKS

The concept of segmentation has its roots in marketing theory. The basis of segmentation as a strategy is that there is no such thing as a homogenous market; consumers differ because of their lifestyles, life chances, expectations and aspirations. Therefore **messages** and symbols will fail to work on all consumers at any one time, thus messages must be made relevant to the target group. The extent to which groups differ is debated. Economists argue that, fundamentally, we are all basically seeking the same goods and services and are largely driven by cost–benefit analysis; this links well to economic theories of voting. Behaviourists refute this, arguing that because any two individuals' cost–benefit analysis will produce contrasting results then the level of service, quality of goods and ergo the cost involved could be far higher. Thus a party can offer a high tax, high spend political programme and find support.

Marketers largely borrow from both camps, as do the majority of political parties that engage in segmentation. While they recognise differences, and develop ways of **narrowcasting** to target groups, these social segments are often large and treated as homogenous independent of their actual structure. This is particularly the case with targeted communication during **election campaigns**, where all voters can receive the message despite it being targeted at one group.

political communication

185

Voter segments are usually determined on the basis of voting behaviour (Bannon, 2003). The best example here of practical segmentation is in the UK and New Labour's targeting of weakly partisan Conservative Party voters; those who would vote Labour but at the time did not. They were given a range of labels: 'Sierra Man' after the popular Ford motor car; 'Basildon Woman' or 'Worcester Woman' named after groups in semi-affluent key constituencies; or the C2s, the aspiring working class. These segments were identified through strategic market intelligence, and then research carried out on their political views. Subsequent communication was mainly targeted at these groups; in the UK in 1997 it was seen that unless these groups supported Labour the party had little chance of winning the election.

Communication will focus on the needs and wants of those voters, using language that they will understand and symbols and rhetoric they will identify with. Advertisements or articles will be placed in 'their' favourite media; often magazines: Tony Blair focused on *Hello, Woman* and *Take A Break* to target 'Worcester Woman'. The purpose of this is shown in Figure 13.

What strategists want to do is communicate with the most important segments in ways that will encourage a positive response. Thus the communication techniques, media and messengers will be designed as a result of research among representatives of that segment. The core aim is to build a sustainable relationship with these voters encouraging mutually beneficial long-term support. Clearly from the diagram, some voters are necessarily ignored, they exist in the wasteland, and if they are not targeted by other political parties can become marginalized from electoral politics.

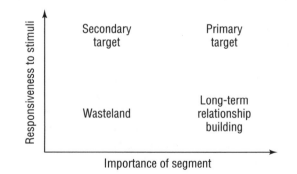

Figure 13   *The process and purpose of segmentation*

key concepts

186

THE ACADEMIC AND PRACTICAL DEBATES

The dealignment of the electorate, and rise of the postmodern political consumer, means that political communication and particularly election campaign communication is difficult to manage. One size no longer fits all and the voter/consumers want messages to be relevant to them. Thus parties have to identify key groups of voters, often those with no partisanship, the floating voters, and aim their key promises towards their wants and needs.

However, outside the USA, few parties have the luxury of access to the resources that targeted advertising demands. While politicians use popular media among target groups, their messages can be further mediated by newspapers or journals with a mass readership. This causes an internal dilemma: does narrowcasting actually alienate core voters if they see messages they do not like? This has been a problem for UK's New Labour. Research shows that the targeting of the affluent suburban middle classes has led to disengagement among their core working-class vote. Evidence for this is shown by the low turnout in Labour safe constituencies at the 2001 general election, as well as by former party members and supporters discussing their perceptions that the parties had changed and no longer represented them (Lilleker, 2005). Studies of smaller parties, such as the Scottish Socialists or a range of left-wing or environmentalist parties across Europe, suggest they are able to target their own voters because of their niche position. However, a mass party finds it difficult to design policies and communication that appeal to broadly contrasting groups, such as middle England as well as those on the poverty line.

FURTHER READING

On voter segmentation by behaviour see D. Bannon (2003) 'Voting, non-voting and consumer buying behaviour: Non-voter segmentation (NVS) and the underlying causes of electoral inactivity', *Journal of Public Affairs*, 3 (2): 138–51. A case study of New Labour's segmentation and its failure among the core voters can be found in D. Lilleker (2005) 'Political marketing: the cause of a democratic deficit?', *Journal of Not-for-profit and Public Sector Marketing*. An overview of segmentation can be found in any marketing textbook, for example Y. Wind's chapter in M. Baker (2000) *Marketing Theory*. London: Thomson. pp. 181–205.

political communication

187

— Soundbite/Soundbite — Culture

> *A soundbite is a line or sentence taken from a longer speech or piece of text that can be used as indicative of the broader content. They are used widely in the media to define an argument, message or policy.*

ORIGINS AND LINKS

The soundbite has always been a feature of media reporting. When a political actor is interviewed, or when they give a statement or produce a manifesto or policy document, sentences are extracted by broadcasters that fit with the framing and agenda of the subsequent report. The length of the soundbite has been reduced drastically over the last four decades since the 1960s, leading political actors to begin inserting them directly into speeches themselves, in an attempt to control the coverage of speeches. Thus a feature of modern speeches is that one brief, vivid phrase may stand out amid much less lucid and more opaque detail; this would be the phrase the writer wants to be inserted into the reports in the media. This is a central feature of modern **news management**.

The politician argued to have first used soundbites in a strategic manner is US President John F. Kennedy; his famous 'Ich bin ein Berliner' (I am a Berliner) spoken to offer his solidarity to West Germans living in the shadow of the Berlin Wall remains paradigmatic of his period of office. In 1964 and 1966 UK Prime Minister Harold Wilson picked up on this style, using it effectively in his first two successful election campaigns. Subsequent political advisors recorded the necessity for devising a 'simple phrase that could be used in speeches, quoted by the media and generally stick in the public mind' (Day, 1982: 8). Over the last two decades since the 1980s soundbites have become a central feature of speeches, subsequent media reports, and are a staple skill required for writing political communication.

KEY FEATURES

The soundbite is central to the notions of professionalised communication. The use of key phrases to attract media attention, and so control coverage, is as much part of the postmodern election and permanent campaign, as leafleting was and is. Any political speech that is publicly available will contain a soundbite, probably several, and it is currently argued that it is impossible for politicians to speak without there being soundbites embedded within their conversation style. While there are exceptions, US President George W. Bush tends to get messages wrong, while UK Deputy Prime Minister John Prescott appears and former Russian President Boris Yeltsin appeared to be in free fall in front of the camera, most political actors appear in control during interviews and intersperse their arguments with memorable phrases designed for posterity. Some argue that soundbites have now become virtually subconscious thoughts made aloud, one example being Tony Blair's well reported, and often pilloried comment: 'this is not a day for soundbites, for today I feel the hand of history upon us', on leaving the Stormont building following the brokering of the Good Friday Agreement, so beginning a ceasefire between Northern Irish paramilitaries. Success can be difficult to measure; however, when considering their use and pick-up rate it can be indicative to locate hard copies of speeches, identify the soundbites and then check the media for their appearance.

THE ACADEMIC AND PRACTICAL DEBATES

Whether soundbites have become a subconscious element of common parlance, or if speechwriters are becoming more skilful at embedding them, almost instantaneously within a statement, is unknown. However, commentators note the rise of a soundbite culture. The obsession with receiving positive news coverage that transmits the right message to the audience means that politicians compete for news coverage through soundbites. Thus political discourse is no more than a meaningless set of rhetorical phrases, each lacking in substance and depth and saying nothing meaningful about actual policy. In this environment, it is argued, there is little wonder that the public are ill-informed, disengaged from electoral politics and cynical when a politician opens his or her mouth.

In their own defence, politicians argue that soundbites are a necessity. If they were to deliver statements in complex, procedural language, listing facts, figures, deadlines or other important information it would just not be reported. They argue that important information is weaved into soundbites, and offered to journalists; it is the media's fault that it is only partially transmitted to the audiences: the soundbite should be the hook on which a range of factual information can be hung. Thus it should act as a heuristic, a point of reference for the audience; however, often it becomes the sole feature of the story without being fully contextualised. This leads journalists and politicians to enter a vicious circle of blame, with both the media and the political communicators seemingly working in opposition to one another despite both relying on the other for news coverage, on the one hand, and news items, on the other. Thus academics studying the use of soundbites recognise them as a common and enduring feature of modern political communication, even if some argue they are unwelcome, unpopular and counter-productive.

FURTHER READING

For an early study of strategic communication in a UK context see B. Day (1982) 'The politics of communication, or the communication of politics', in R. Worcester and M. Harrop, *Political Communications: The British General Election of 1979*. London: Allen & Unwin. A broader history, focusing mainly on the UK but with comparative examples, is M. Rosenbaum (1997) *From Soapbox to Soundbite: Party Political Campaigning in Britain since 1945*. Basingstoke: Macmillan. A critique of the use of soundbites, and of the emerging soundbite culture can be found in D. Slayden, R.K. Whillock and R. Kirk (eds) (1999) *Soundbite Culture: The Death of Discourse in a Wired World*. Thousand Oaks, CA: Sage.

Source–Reporter Relations

Source–reporter relations describe the relationship, formal or informal, between the journalist and the source of news information, in this context the politician or their employed representative.

The term comes from the study of journalism, and is normally focused on from the perspective of the journalist or reporter. However, it is recognised that there is a dynamic of power between the source and the reporter. One needs access to the news, the other requires information; however, while these goals seem complimentary, the source may have a range of other objectives for gaining access to the news and its **audience** and uses a range of **news management** techniques to realise them. With the **professionalisation** of political communication, **spin-doctors** use more and more sophisticated methods for getting their **message** across. The success of these techniques, however, can be heavily reliant on the media and the likelihood that mass media outlets will transmit political organisations' messages to their audience.

KEY FEATURES

The development of media–political relations, spin-doctoring and the journalist response to this has shaped modern political source–reporter relations. First, focusing on the issue of media/press–party parallelism: at one time in recent history the media was largely controlled by party members or came under the direct control of government. This remains a feature of emergent democracies of eastern Europe (Milton, 2000), as it was in France under President De Gaulle and to some extent during the Second World War in the UK. For the most part, this era is over and now parties have little control over the media; thus they have to resort to news management techniques. The use of spin has a number of features, but relates mainly to the way that messages are framed to satisfy news values. They are designed to anticipate the strategies of opponents, and the information is subsidised to give a positive impression of the sender.

Arguably this is a reaction to the evolution of a new type of journalist, what Barnett (2002) refers to as the Rottweiler or Sabato (1991) describes in similar terms as the junk-yard dog. For them, this style of journalist attacks the source, usually in a public forum such as a news magazine programme, as well as seeking out controversial stories such as intra-party divisions or evidence of sleaze and corruption. This is far removed from the tradition of deference which political actors enjoyed up to the 1980s, when they were treated with respect by media interviewers. The evolution of the source–reporter relations, in relation to the three key aspects is illustrated in Table 4.

political communication

191

Table 4 *The evolution of source–reporter relations*

Press–party parallelism (Negrine, 1989)	Typology of media's role	Party communication strategies
Organisational Formal and informal links/affiliations	Informer/educator provides information editors believe to be important in an objective, bland format Editorials will support party loyally without question News can highlight one party over another.	Product-oriented Use of interpersonal as well as media. Value-driven aimed at partisans, some persuasion to floating voters
Goal-oriented parallelism Sharing political or ideological stance, editorial support	Watchdog Offers electoral loyalty, but is not partisan unquestioningly	Sales-oriented Aimed at both the media and voters. Focus on partisan media organisations for free publicity
Readership orientation No loyalty. Can lean towards a party if the readers are supportive Follows trends	Entertainer Market-oriented and so interested in what the audience wants. Delivers infotainment and can report politics in the same way as celebrity news	Market-oriented Focused on voter. Seek to control messages and their packaging, use professional news managers

Journalists happily blame the changes on politicians and their use of spin, politicians in turn blame the attack journalism on the necessity for spin; hence both enter into a game of blame and counter-blame. This less than edifying spectacle is argued to contribute to public disengagement from politics and the interest in infotainment.

THE ACADEMIC AND PRACTICAL DEBATES

The key question, debated particularly in the UK and US, is whither the relationship between the media and the political sphere. While some argue that the attack and counter-attack actually fuels public interest, so creating a virtuous circle that results in higher public engagement (Norris, 2000), voting figures and measures of trust in both politicians and journalists suggest the reverse is the case. Turnout is in steady decline, on average about 50 per cent across all nations that have voluntary participation in elections, while at the same time around 10 per cent of the public say that neither journalists nor politicians can be trusted. Therefore we may argue that there is, in fact, a vicious circle in operation. Politicians use spin and communicative subterfuge, which then becomes the media story rather than higher political issues. This obsession with process reduces the efficacy of the system, thus reinforcing arguments for politicians to use more spin; and so the relationship spirals out of control.

Norris (2000) notes that America is an exception, that surveys suggest the US electorate are not all engaged by the 'heated and conflictual' politics that were a feature of the 1960s and beyond. However, given the discussions of Americanisation, perhaps actually the trend towards disengagement is hidden in many of the European nations featured in Norris's study. Similarly, the tradition of spin matched with attack journalism is not yet prevalent across all democracies; it is more a feature of the UK post-1997 than elsewhere. This is an area of increasing interest, one that is argued to have the most profound effect on the public interface with politics, but is still evolving. We may yet see a return to a more consensual relationship, as few wish to consider the complete breakdown in relations between government and the media.

FURTHER READING

On the virtuous circle and the evolution of party communication see P. Norris (2000) *Virtuous Circle*. London: Cambridge University Press; an alternative view is presented in D. Lilleker, R. Negrine and J. Stanyer (2003) 'Vicious circle', *Politics Review*, 2 (3): 6–9. A good introduction to the relations between state and media, both ideal and real, can be found in A. Milton (2000) *The Rational Politician: Exploiting the Media in New Democracies*. London: Ashgate; or L. Larsson (2002) 'Journalists and politicians: a relationship requiring manoeuvring space', *Journalism Studies*, 3 (1): 21–33. On the evolution of journalist practice see S. Barnett (2002) 'Will a crisis in journalism provoke a crisis in democracy', *The Political Quarterly*, 73 (4): 400–8; L. Sabato (1991) *Feeding Frenzy: How Attack Journalism has Transformed American Politics*. New York: Free Press.

political communication

Spin/Spin-Doctor

The term **spin** is used to denote media management techniques that hinder journalists from reporting news objectively and from accessing all the information. The **spin-doctor** is an individual who attempts to use spin to influence public opinion by placing a favourable bias on information presented to the public, usually via the media.

ORIGINS AND LINKS

Spin is characterised by Moloney (2001) as an exchange or contest between information and publicity, where politicians attempt to impart the former and gain the latter at the same time. The term comes not from academia but from the realm of sport: specifically cricket and baseball. Spin is what a professional bowler, or pitcher, will apply to a ball to prevent the batsman from sending it in the direction desired; it causes the ball to leave the bat in an unexpected trajectory, hopefully making it easier for a fielder to catch. Although slightly lacking fit to political communication in this form, it was adopted as a descriptive term by the *New York Times* when covering the presidential election of 1984. Since then it has become common parlance, as well as practice. We understand it to mean the way in which the 'spin-doctor', or media management consultant, attempts to control the media agenda: 'moulding the images we see and crafting the words we hear'. They basically attempt to prevent the journalist from doing their job in the same way that a spin bowler prevents the batsman performing correctly.

The concept of spin, however, has become quite postmodern. After all, there is no truth. Realities are a matter of perception, they are created and destroyed and only exist at an individual level. Just as films, soap operas, popular music or fiction can create realities, such as norms of society, a spin-doctor will attempt to manufacture a reality regarding government policy, a party's cohesion or the achievement of targets. The reality that is constructed is one of imagery, **packaging**, designer politics and **aestheticisation**. However, on a more devious level, it is also about

information subsidies and the obscuration of truth; such as the burying of bad news under the events of 9/11, as was suggested by Jo Moore, communications consultant in the UK's Department of Transport.

KEY FEATURES

It is appropriate to discuss here the qualities that are expected of a spin-doctor, and the skills and tasks involved. First, it is important to note that the spin-doctor is far more than a public relations expert or propagandist; their role is that of an aide. Clinton's relationship with James Carville, and similarly the perceived reliance of Tony Blair on Alastair Campbell, suggests it is more than just media myth when these individuals are classed as 'the deputy'. The problem in both the US and the UK, however, is that spin has become the story and spin-doctors the celebrities. While this appears key to recognising when spin is being utilised, in fact the opposite is the case.

Spin and its doctor should be invisible, not necessarily out of the view of the camera, but their practice should go unnoticed. In the UK we hear stories of Peter Mandelson and Alastair Campbell bullying reporters from both the BBC and ITV, while in France and Germany it is only academics that take an interest in the spin-doctor. This may not be culturally or contextually specific, rather that the spin-doctors that do exist are doing a better job, and perhaps in a less hostile environment, than their UK/US counterparts. In the modern 24/7 media environment, with fewer journalists working to tighter deadlines, the spin-doctor should be the journalist's ally; making life easier for them. One advisory text argues 'briefings and press conferences [should] serve as a watering hole for packs of journalists in search of news', but instead, as former BBC journalist Nicholas Jones recalls of briefings in the UK by the Prime Minister's official spokesperson, they became hostile affairs. This is characteristic of the breakdown in political source–reporter relations in the UK; elsewhere we do not hear of such hostilities or, largely, of the spin-doctors.

However, spin is not simply the preserve of the political communications strategy. An example of spin in action can be used to demonstrate its usage by the media also, a game of spin and counter-spin, in the official and media reporting of the case for war against Iraq in the UK in September 2002. The Labour government report *Iraq's Weapons of Mass Destruction*, now universally regarded as the 'dodgy dossier', contained a number of facts that subsequently were shown to be not wholly accurate. While debates continue surrounding the complicity of the government in misleading parliament and the public, and regarding the extent to which intelligence was flawed, one statement was selected to highlight the threat posed by Saddam Hussein's Iraq. That statement was that Iraq possessed weapons of mass destruction that could hit British interests in 45 minutes. Without entering into debates on the accuracy, it is clear that this was not a clear presentation of facts, but a sensationalist way of demonstrating a threat existed that would attract significant media attention.

While the UK media indeed picked up on that statement, allegations made on BBC Radio Four's *Today* programme the following June that the document had been sexed up by Downing Street equally did not present the full facts. First, there was only one source for that allegation and second, that person did not have access to the workings of the Downing Street communications machine. The death of the source, Dr David Kelly, a scientist within the Ministry of Defence specialising in weapons of mass destruction, and enquiry into the circumstances leading up to his death found guilt on both sides; though the BBC was seen as most complicit. However, from a perspective of information provision we see both sides as being at fault in withholding vital facts that could have aided the public to make an informed conclusion on whether war was the proper course of action.

THE ACADEMIC AND PRACTICAL DEBATES

The need for spin in the UK is argued to be the rise of the Rottweiler journalist, the investigative reporter that is out to savage the ill-prepared, non-media savvy political actor. Thus professional communication consultants are employed to manage relations with the media. Elsewhere, the requirement to communicate professionally is cited. However, many argue the negative consequences are too high a price to pay.

The breakdown in source–reporter relations, culminating in the fight surrounding the dodgy dossier detailing the threat posed by Iraq in 2002, subsequent damning of the document as being 'sexed-up' by Campbell, and the suicide of scientist Dr David Kelly the man who made this claim, resulted in the Hutton Inquiry. This inquiry, regarded by parts of the media as a whitewash, found the BBC guilty of being overly critical of the government, actively seeking grounds for attack, and thus relying on a single source: the ill-fated Kelly. However, a further consequence was the proclamation of the death of spin. Campbell resigned from 10 Downing Street and communications became lower profile. But spin remains a feature of democratic systems, albeit hidden under the guise of media relations. The circumstances surrounding the death of Dr Kelly, resulting in the Hutton Inquiry, is a shocking example of the result of losing spin, the spiralling mistrust between media and government, yet it currently is a very British problem. Debates currently focus on the necessity for spin, whether it is appropriate for democratic pluralism and if spin is in fact dead in the post-Hutton UK and Bush's US and the broader democratic world.

FURTHER READING

A history of the 'rise and fall' of the use of spin is documented in G. Pitcher (2002) *The Death of Spin*. London: John Wiley. Spin under Clinton in the US is detailed in H. Kurtz (1998) *Spin Cycle: Inside the Clinton Propaganda Machine*. New York: Free Press; a UK case study is presented in K. Moloney (2001) 'The rise and fall of spin: Changes of fashion in the presentation of UK politics' *Journal of Public Affairs*, 1 (2): 124–35; for a more comparative analysis see F. Esser, C. Reinemann and D. Fan (2001) 'Spin-doctors in the United States, Great Britain, and Germany: Metacommunication about media manipulation', *Harvard International Journal of Press/Politics*, 6 (1): 16–45.

Technological Determinism

Technological determinism is the idea that technology is the determining factor, or driving force, behind the professionalisation of political communication.

197

ORIGINS AND LINKS

As political leaders adapt their styles of communication to television, and leaders are judged on their televisual skill, it seems a simple truism that television has changed political communication. As greater reliance is placed on the television by politicians keen to 'enter the homes of voters', they are driven to become 'media savvy', use soundbites, package their news stories to fit the values of the programme, and perform well on camera. As technology alters, providing, first, 24/7 news coverage and live access to the public and, secondly, an unmediated mode of communication via the World Wide Web, politicians are seen to adapt to employing that technology. Thus the plethora of political websites, web logs, e-newsletters and a variety of other virtual communications provide evidence of technology again shaping the behaviour of the political organisations.

KEY FEATURES

Key to understanding the way in which political organisations adapt to technology is represented in Downes and Mui's law of disruption (2000). This recognises that commercial organisations are the first to seize new technologies and exploit their potential. By offering attractive goods and services to the public, the commercial users draw in an audience, thus broadening the appeal of the medium and making it attractive to other organisations wishing to communicate to society. Among these organisations are the political parties and pressure groups, each seeking to maximise the potential of the new communication tools. However, for political organisations, adaptation is slower, investment is usually lower and they often measure the gains against the risks far less strategically.

THE ACADEMIC AND PRACTICAL DEBATES

While it seems to make sense that political organisations adapt their communications to all technologies available, we should ask whether technology is the sole driving factor. Technological determinists would argue that it is; however, that position is critiqued by social determinism. As we note from Downes and Mui's analysis (2000), it is the public use of technology that led to its potential being explored by political organisations. Therefore, we can see that as radio was surpassed as the key mass media for reaching large audiences, television became the key medium for political actors. However, if radio remained a trusted source of information, this may have retained prominence instead of being a secondary communication tool. Thus society is argued to drive changes in the mode of communication to a far greater extent than the fact that technology exists to facilitate new forms of communication.

Technological Determinism

Introductions to the topic are offered in M. R. Smith and L. Marx (1994) *Does Technology Drive History? The Dilemma of Technological Determinism.* Cambridge, MA: MIT Press; D. MacKenzie (1999) 'Technological determinism', in W.H. Dutton (ed.), *Society on the Line: Information Politics in the Digital Age.* Oxford: Oxford University Press. pp. 39–41. The changes facilitated and lead by television are explored in Martin Rosenbaum (1996) *From Soapbox to Soundbite.* Basingstoke: Macmillan; see on social and technological determinism L. Downes and C. Mui (2000) *Unleashing the Killer App.* Boston, MA: Harvard University Press. The potential and usage of the Web is discussed by N. Jackson (2003) 'MPs and web technologies – an untapped opportunity?', *Journal of Public Affairs*, 3 (2): 124–37.

Terrorism

Terrorism is the forcing of issues onto the political and news agenda by creating a climate of fear, usually relating to one single demonstration of power by the terrorist organisation. In the context of 11 September 2001 it could easily be described as the most powerful and influential form of political communication.

political communication

199

ORIGINS AND LINKS

Terrorism, famously, is a misnomer. This is exemplified with the adage 'one man's terrorist is another man's freedom fighter', an observation that relates well to groups such as the IRA; ETA, the Basque separatist movement; and indeed the Muslim fundamentalist groups of which al-Qaeda is currently the most famous or infamous. Terrorism, however, should actually be treated as being a part of a long-standing tradition of direct action: action taken by groups who have no access to the news agenda under normal circumstances. These groups are marginalized from accessing the **public sphere**, usually for political–economic motives, and so resort to tactics that shock, grab media attention and so set the news **agenda**.

The key difference between terrorism and much direct political action is its ability to 'outrage the community', not just the one under attack, but the broader community. While al-Qaeda shocked the western world, as have the IRA, Germany's Bader-Meinhoff group and the Palestine Liberation Organisation (PLO), most direct action will only shock the community they attack. Environmentalist or animal rights groups often have broad support and are only categorised as terrorists by those who suffer their attacks. Their actions are designed to circumnavigate the **hegemony** of ideas, set **news values** and control the agenda, so prioritising their **message** above those of other political organisations inside a society.

KEY FEATURES

Terrorism is simply shock tactics. It is caused by the marginalisation of groups usually through the military or economic power of nations or groups of nations. The IRA fought what it described as 'English imperialism'; the PLO fought the Jewish State of Israel for independence; al-Qaeda and its allies fight 'western economic imperialism' within the Middle East. It is almost uniformly linked to actions that cause the loss of life, such as 9/11, the bombings on Madrid commuter trains in 2004, the Real IRA's bombing of Omagh in 1999 or the bomb attacks on the London transport system during July 2005.

THE ACADEMIC AND PRACTICAL DEBATES

While these events are seen as cataclysmic, receive widespread news coverage and can cause negative coverage of both the perpetrators and those whom they seek to gain freedom from, it is questionable whether terrorism works. As Schmid and de Graaf (1982) found, while the action may be reported, from then on the news agenda is set by the 'opponents': 'the government and its security forces', not by the terrorist. Because they are secretive groups they have little access to the media. While this is changing, largely due to the free and open access permitted by the Internet, so allowing the terrorist groups in Iraq to publicise their execution of hostages, and the access also permitted to them by Al-Jazeera the Qatar TV station for the Arab world, mainstream access is still largely limited.

Therefore, despite needing to demonstrate their capability to hurt their enemy, while also publicising the injustices they have faced, any successes may well be pyrrhic. The events of 9/11 have led to a reduction in sympathy for Arab and Muslim causes, and to public support being gained for a number of military expeditions, against firstly the Taliban regime in Afghanistan and then against Iraq. Though the media may report some of the background to the terrorist attacks, the agenda soon shifts away from them on to their victims and then the war against them. Thus, as McNair (2003) notes, 'much media coverage of terrorism may be viewed as self-defeating'.

FURTHER READING

The seminal work in this area is A. Schmid and J. de Graaf (1982) *Violence as Communication*. London: Sage. For a recent debate see B. McNair (2003) *An Introduction to Political Communication*. London: Routledge. pp. 181–6. A plethora of works have looked at al-Qaeda post 9/11: a good example is P. Berger (2001) *Holy War Inc*. New York: Simon and Schuster.

Uses and Gratifications Theory

Uses and gratifications theory seeks to explain the way in which audiences interpret mass communication. Unlike many theories that describe the audience as passive receivers who are easily manipulated, here we find that audiences use communication for their own purposes and seek gratifications from that use. So, audience members may well watch a political advert to discover only what that party is saying on one issue; say education. They will then use the information in other aspects of their life, for example they may be teachers or school governors, and assess whether that party is offering something that they like or not, and further along decide whether to offer their support to the party. Uses and gratifications theory suggests we select the bits of communication we wish to hear, ignore that which we do not want to hear, and use communication to satisfy our own needs. If this is the case then it shifts power away from the sender to the receiver in a fairly dramatic way.

ORIGINS AND LINKS

Uses and gratifications theory emerged from the study of **audience** behaviour in terms of watching television or selecting a newspaper. It attempted to explain the complexities behind choices made on an everyday basis. Its application to politics is still in its infancy and there remain some practical difficulties. While it is both a persuasive and a useful way of explaining how audiences translate and mentally interact with mass communication, it does not allow for effects upon the audience, only on the **messages** received. As the majority of political communication involves a degree of persuasion, this means that the theory can only at best describe half the story; it can explain how messages are interpreted but not always whether they are influential and why. A further weakness is that it does not explicitly allow for **ideology** to govern our choices. An audience member loyal to one party may be far more inclined to listen to politicians of that party, watch their broadcasts and read their leaflets. The use here would be to reinforce their political beliefs, and they may well get gratification from that reinforcement. However, it is harder to explain how individuals allow alternative views into their lives. Uses and gratifications theory suggests these would be blocked out; however, this is difficult to do when faced with the myriad forms of political communication that often will offer directly competing views simultaneously. Here we should think about the **mediatisation** of political speeches, the various debate shows that offer rival accounts, or the way that **news values** influence the **framing** of news stories. These aspects of the communication of politics mean that uses and gratifications theory is a useful tool for explaining some aspects of our field of study only.

Studies employing uses and gratifications theory to explain audience engagement with political communication have, however, attempted to circumnavigate these problems by focusing on voters with weak ideological beliefs and consequent weak ties to political parties. These floating voters are often hungry for as much information as is possible to allow them to make the right decision on election day. Thus audience members interpret political communication to make it relevant to their own lives, to assess the strengths and weaknesses of the competitors and so to determine their electoral choice.

KEY FEATURES

Any society where audiences can be analysed using uses and gratifications theory must be one that is information rich. Therefore pluralism cannot just be an ideal but a reality. We would expect, and academic studies have focused on, a vast variety of political information sources, not only traditional mass media, but narrowcast direct communication and use of the Internet for news gathering and for accessing party and candidate websites and related materials. Aligned to this we would need a preponderance of floating voters: those who would need to be accessing a wide array of information in order to participate in voting in a meaningful, informed and self-satisfying way. Without these features we cannot apply the theory at all.

With these features in place within society, we would then expect people to be politically aware and interested, to be accessing the political information available to them, and for research to show that this contributes to voter decision making.

THE ACADEMIC AND PRACTICAL DEBATES

Unlike many of the concepts introduced, uses and gratifications theory is applied by academics in hindsight. Voters are tested on their accessing of information and the way that this subsequently affects their choice in the voting booth. The earliest study, carried out in the UK by Jay Blumler and Denis McQuail, found that close attention to television coverage of the 1964 general election was able to change perceptions of party leaders and the abilities of parties to govern (Blumler and McQuail, 1968). They used their findings to argue for the media to present more, good quality, information particularly giving airtime to programmes that allow the leaders to showcase their abilities and arguments. This, they argued, would be of more use to those voters seeking political information and allow them to make more informed choices. More recent work, derived from the Cologne Election Study of 1995, found voter expectations for receiving information were high. This research also found that receiving information often provided voters with the incentive to be more proactive in seeking additional information (Ohr and Schott, 2001). Therefore, modern voters would not simply rely on the television for their news but would seek information on parties and candidates from a variety of other sources; including the Internet. Research has shown that subscribers to party e-newsletters equally can be viewed as fitting with a uses and gratifications approach: respondents to a 2004 online survey in the UK claimed that one key reason for subscribing to the e-newsletter was for deciding who to vote for in a forthcoming election.

Therefore, despite some of the problems with adapting a mass communication theory to political communication, we find that this can be used to explain the behaviour of voters who are seeking information to guide their political choice but who have no predetermined political views. With the expansion of **dealignment**, this could then be influential in shaping the provision of information and the style of future political communication.

FURTHER READING

For the earliest study of political communication using uses and gratifications theory see J. Blumler and D. McQuail (1968) *Television in Politics*. London: Faber & Faber). The recent study of German voters is D. Ohr and P.R. Schott (2001) 'Campaigns and information seeking: Evidence from a German state election', *European Journal of Communication*, 16 (4): 419–49. A contemporary introduction is provided in Lynda Lee Kaid (2004) *Handbook of Political Communication Research*. New York: Lawrence Erlbaum.

Virtual Politics/ Virtual Communities

Virtual politics is political activity that takes place on the Internet in virtual space and time; communities of shared interest are created to deal with specific issues, to support particular political ideas or to raise awareness.

ORIGINS AND LINKS

The notion of there being virtual communities active in virtual political activity is not solely a feature of the Internet. Many groups in history have existed outside the public sphere while still contributing efficiently to it and often become instrumental in causing political change. Revolutionary groups, support groups and issue-based political organisations have all existed, run by a small cadre, but having the ability to call on a mass of people to take part in demonstrations of the organisation's power. One example is the global Aid to Russia movement that collected masses of blankets, food and equipment to aid the besieged Russian people during the German invasion of 1942–44. The movement grew from groups of sympathisers, often communists, in non-occupied countries all acting independently at the local level. Only when the quantity of aid collected exceeded expectations did national organisations, particularly trade unions, become involved to coordinate getting supplies to the areas where they were needed. What the Internet has provided is the facility to create a global community, still with a loose organisational structure, but which operates on the will of its members.

These virtual communities exist in many forms and for many purposes. There are a range of consumerist organisations, where consumers who buy online can exchange ideas and comments, as well as goods, and therefore can influence the marketing process (Hemetsberger, 2002). Equally often talked of communities are those that share files over the Internet, usually in MP3 format. However, political groups are also exploiting the potential of the Internet, not just as a political tool but as a way of cutting through the noise, avoiding media gatekeepers, and gaining direct access to an audience. Some argue this represents a new public sphere, a more open one to that of the bourgeois cafés suggested by Habermas, one that facilitates a greater sense of public representation, that allows a space for a global community to exist, exchanging ideas and breaking down social, historical, cultural and political barriers. This is clearly an idealised picture; however, evidence does suggest that virtual political and social communities do exist and that they have some impact, at the very least upon their members (see Figure 14, which shows a website that offers a range of ways to interact with anarchists in the Washington, DC area as well as on a more global scale).

KEY FEATURES

Communication using information communication technology (ICT) has revolutionised access to the public sphere in at least one important way, that is, that there is no such thing as control over information. Any individual with a personal computer, a modem, a service provider and a telephone line can access a global community. While clearly there are educational and resource issues that restrict access, in theory the Internet is open and available to all. In times of war the accessibility is perhaps clearest. As Belgrade was bombed by NATO to force the Serbian

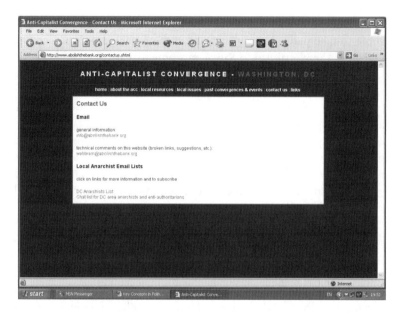

Figure 14   *The Anti-Capitalist Convergence website*

government to withdraw troops from Kosovo, ordinary Serbians sent emails to contacts in the UK and USA to relay their personal experiences. Many of these found their way onto the pages of popular newspapers and became mainstream news items of their own. These offered accounts that no embedded journalist or war correspondent could, and so they were highly newsworthy. More recently the Baghdad blogger found similar fame for giving personal, insider views of the future of postwar Iraq. These examples demonstrate the power of the Internet in bringing the global population closer together; however, these are individuals, not communities.

Communities are far harder to create, but the practice of blogging (creating a web-based diary or log) which is accessible to all and can be commented on allows individuals to interact on a range of diverse subjects. Former US actor Wil Wheaton comments on a range of topics from his career in *Star Trek: The Next Generation*, to his family life, to election campaigning in the USA. Elsewhere, a Dutch student calling himself 'Dood' made a comment about every Dutch party leader on 21 January the day before the 2003 Dutch general election. This one entry received 114 comments, some congratulatory, some in opposition and some that made little sense, but each one could be accessed, read, and commented on. Often, this can result in a debate surrounding one offhand remark that managed to capture the interest of the global audience.

Such communications can lead to the creation of a community. Members can access at their leisure, as regularly as they wish and at a time convenient for them. Research into virtual consumer communities discusses the motivations of participants and their expressed goals. These are easily translated into a political context, as is demonstrated in Table 5.

Table 5   *Motivations and rewards from participating in virtual politics*

Action	Motive/Reward	Level of Participation
Joining	Involvement Empowerment	Finding you are not alone Gaining knowledge
Offering comments	Social approval: recognition Gaining contacts	Finding a voice: desire to be listened to Passive contributions
Exchanging views	Moral obligation Belonging	Active contribution
Setting common tasks and goals	Shared passions Shared values	Communal decision making Interaction
Community building	Drive to change things	Intimate communal ties Sharing of knowledge Building of trust

Those who join, often start off by lurking on the edge of communities and refusing to actively participate; hence they are known as 'lurkers'. However, it is argued that before long many move towards giving voice to their concerns, entering into exchanges of views, setting down common tasks and goals for the community and helping to build a community that operates both virtually and 'in the real world'. Evidence for this is shown in Rodgers's study of peace movements in Yorkshire and Alaska, who exchanged ideas for campaigns and created a solidarity network (Rodgers, 2003). Similar communities were created following the Asian tsunami, for example the SEA-EAT blog, created by Paola di Maio, a survivor in Phuket, and his Internet contact Peter Griffin, an Indian-based IT consultant, and became the tenth most visited humanitarian site on the Internet in four days. The SEA-EAT website basically publicised the stories of the people of the region, and became an unofficial resource for

political communication

people whose loved ones were missing as well as a focus for individuals seeking information on the effects of the Tsunami; including journalists and aid workers. The question is, do these sites actually affect political decision making, or are they simply used for personal information gathering?

THE ACADEMIC AND PRACTICAL DEBATES

While there are those, such as Rodgers (2003), who herald these virtual communities as a new dimension for political activity or, like Sinikka Sassi (2001), who talk of the transformation of the public sphere, others are more cautious. In a discussion of where the public, private and political spheres converge, John Corner (2003) argues that the Internet is simply one further location for political communication. Just as the public may discuss politics in cafés, bars and lounges across the nations, they also use the Internet. Here they may well seek specialist information, establish links to organisations with an ideological position that they share, or find ways to express their political views; however, this may not suggest a fundamental shift away from traditional political behaviour among either the public or the political organisations.

The reasons for this centre on the debate surrounding what it is that the Internet offers. Does it offer a fundamentally new form of communication, or is it actually just a new way of doing old practices? Clearly the Internet allows people from across continents to communicate with each other in real time; while communication has often crossed frontiers during wars the delays were massive and lines of communication unreliable. While many wars have diarists able to send messages from behind or between the lines, such immediate and unedited insights are only possible through the development and proliferation of the Internet. It also facilitates instant access to environments that previously would have been unreachable, such as an area hit by the tsunami within hours of it striking. But does any of this change the way politics is conducted.

The simple answer is probably, but it is hard to say how. In the case of the bombing of Belgrade it was a further voice of criticism that the NATO member governments had to respond to. With the Baghdad blogger, he became more of a media performer than a political voice. However, some other virtual communities have a direct effect on the public consciousness. The organisations which rallied against capitalism, demonstrating spectacularly against the World Bank and meetings of the World Trade Organisation, made a very public impact by capturing the news agenda. While they may not have changed policy they made the public aware of their arguments. Similarly the Stop the War Coalition captured the headlines with protests against the war on Iraq. These demonstrations were facilitated by the Internet; it is truly a new way to organise established tactics, but also appears to offer a way to create a stronger, more active, and more cohesive activist base.

Such examples go against the idea of the web-user being a solitary and insular being collecting information for their own uses and gratifications. Instead it suggests a community spirit exists that some of these individuals buy into when it suits. Marketing experts have found that the Internet is limited in terms of its potential for selling, a lesson that established political organisations perhaps need to take on board. Instead the web-user seeks social interaction on a broader scale than is the case in what we could call their 'real world'. They wish to form relationships, bonds and ties with each other and with organisations: in the words of one report the Internet is full of 'partners on whom you can rely and with whom you can act' (Rushkoff, 2003). Rushkoff's report suggest that politics needs to change to meet the needs of this new consumer who expects that political organisations should be more keen to build such relationships than the corporate organisations that actually are. This is at present an ideal; however, the levels of political interaction that take place on the Internet does suggest there is truth in the predictions Rushkoff offers.

FURTHER READING

On the role of the web for consumer culture see A. Hemetsberger (2002) 'Fostering cooperation in the Internet: social exchange processes in innovative virtual consumer communities', in S.M. Broniarczyk and K. Nakamoto, *Advances in Consumer Research*, vol. 29. pp. 354–6 (available at www.vancouver.wsu.edu/acr/home.htm). The changing face of political communication is explored in J. Corner (2003) 'Mediated persona and political culture', in J. Corner and D. Pels, *Media and the Restyling of Politics*. London: Sage; J. Rodgers (2003) *Spatializing International Politics: Analysing Activism on the Internet*. London: Routledge; S. Sassi (2001) 'The transformation of the public sphere', in B. Axford and R. Huggins, *New Media and Politics*. London: Sage. An idealist view of the future of politics is offered in D. Rushkoff (2003) *Open Source Democracy: How Online Communication is Changing Offline Politics*. London: Demos. For blogs search the web, there are thousands out there.

political communication

209